PRAISE FOR HORSES, LOVE & SCIENCE

> Congratulations to Meg Kirby on creating a book that explores the world of horsemanship, equine-assisted therapy, and mental health! It is evident that Meg has poured her hunger, heart, and hard work into this book. I believe the book can be helpful for both novice and experienced horse-riders who wish to deepen their understanding of the human-horse relationship by becoming a conscious, aware horseperson. The practical insights and exercises in this book can help readers increase awareness and develop an intentional relationship with their horses. Overall, "Horses, Love & Science: The Eight Commitments of I-Thou Horsepersonship" is a valuable resource for anyone not only interested in training their horse but also in developing themselves.

Marijke de Jong,
Founder of The Straightness Training Academy

> Horses, Love and Science captures the sensitivity of the relationship between horses and their riders or handlers. Meg Kirby brilliantly uses Buber's I-Thou philosophy to underpin the essence of working within the realm of horses' individuality that allows the reader to see horses as beings with intrinsic value, paving the way to a profound sense of relationship and personal growth. The Eight Commitments provide a solid roadmap to the art of horsepersonship that reveals the beautiful interspecies bond that can be formed. Whether you are new to or advanced in equine-assisted services or horsepersonship, this book will ignite your soul and guide you to a deeper understanding of the horse-human relationship.

Amy Johnson, Animal-Assisted Services Researcher,
Educator and Practitioner, University of North Florida

> Meg Kirby's I-Thou Horsepersonship and its Eight Commitments provide a wonderful superstructure for anyone seeking to understand and evolve their interactions with horses. Anchored in whole-individual and humanistic approaches, this book will help you relate to horses and to yourself in trauma-informed and value-centred ways.

Nina Ekholm Fry, MSSC., CCTP, Director of Equine Programs,
Institute for Human-Animal Connection, University of Denver

> *My goal is to operationalise this way of being with horses, training horses, learning with horses and learning from horses as simply as I can. It is a kind, loving, safe and simple approach, where horses have their species-specific needs met, and where horses benefit from the relationship with people.*

HORSES, LOVE & SCIENCE

The Eight Commitments of I-Thou Horsepersonship

MEG KIRBY

Aware Publishing

First published in Australia 2023 by Meg Kirby.

Copyright © 2023 Meg Kirby. All rights reserved.

The moral rights of the author have been asserted.

National Library of Australia Cataloguing in Publications data:

Author: Meg Kirby

Title: Horses, Love & Science: The Eight Commitments of I-Thou Horsepersonship

 A catalogue record for this book is available from the National Library of Australia

Subject: Horses, Horsemanship, Horse Training, Equitation Science, Equine Assisted Therapy, Psychotherapy, Mental Health, Equine Assisted Psychotherapy

ISBN: 978-0-6450621-6-8 (Paperback) & 978-0-6450621-7-5 (eBook)

Cover photo and internal photo credit: Cailin Rose

Thank you to Monique Curtis for featuring in images throughout.

Disclaimer: The material in this publication is of the nature of general comment only and does not represent professional advice. It is not intended to provide specific guidance for particular circumstances and should not be relied on as the basis for any decision to take action or not take action on any matters it covers. Readers should obtain professional advice as appropriate before taking any action. To the maximum extent permitted by law, the author and publisher disclaim all responsibility and liability to any person, arising directly or indirectly from any person taking or not taking action based on the information in this book.

DEDICATION

I dedicate this book to my beautiful daughters, Rose and Jasmine. You will recognise my love for Horses in my deep love for You both, above all, and for all Animals. Each day I feel grateful and amazed at how lucky I am to have such incredibly funny, gorgeous, intelligent and talented daughters in my life. I love my Life so much, partly, because I get to Live it with you both. You Inspire me. Our family life together has always included our animal-friends (equine, canine, feline, leporidae & macropod) and even though you like to sometimes make fun of my obsession (with horses, animals, and animal welfare) I know you both understand and share a deep empathy with animals.

I also want to dedicate this book to Valence Williams and Paula Jewell. From very early days working together, I knew you both *understood* I-Thou relating with horses and animals. Both of you are more talented with horses and animals (respectively), than I will ever be. You both have a humility, passion, kindness and skill with horses and animals, that is a rare treasure indeed. Thank you.

Meg Kirby

ABOUT THE AUTHOR

Meg Kirby is an Author, Founder, Director and Senior Trainer at The Equine Psychotherapy Institute and Animal Assisted Psychotherapy International, Mental Health Social Worker, and Gestalt Psychotherapist of over 25 years. Meg is Founder of I-Thou Horsepersonship and I-Thou Inter-Species Relating, championing an ethical and aware relationship with Horses and all Animals.

Meg is passionate about supporting people and animals to experience freedom and wellbeing. She helps people to trust the wisdom of their body, feelings and whole-being, and to fall in love with Life, with the support and wisdom from horses, all animals and nature.

Meg began working in Child and Adolescent Psychiatry and Mental Health Inpatient and Outpatient Units, before moving to Adult Mental Health Therapeutic Community practice and working with Dual Diagnosis and Complex Needs, and finally settling into Private Practice as a Psychotherapist incorporating room-based, equine assisted, animal assisted, and nature assisted psychotherapy for children, adults, couples, families, and organisations. During this time, Meg developed a unique way of living, relating and learning with horses and other animals.

In 2011, Meg created and founded *The Equine Psychotherapy Institute*, offering Australia's first independent training pathway and comprehensive model of practice for students looking for robust education in equine assisted psychotherapy (for registered mental health professionals) and equine assisted learning (for teachers, animal-based professionals, coaches, and disability workers). In 2020, Meg founded *Animal Assisted Psychotherapy International* as a specialised branch of The Equine Psychotherapy Institute, offering a comprehensive year-long training pathway for international and Australian students to learn the depth of Animal Assisted Psychotherapy and Animal Assisted Learning, from a humanistic psychotherapy and I-Thou Inter-species Relating lens.

Meg published her first book in 2016, "An Introduction to Equine Assisted Psychotherapy: principles, theory and practice of the Equine Psychotherapy Institute Model". She has since authored a second book, "Equine Therapy Exposed: Real Life Case Studies of Equine Assisted Psychotherapy and Equine Assisted Learning with Everyday People and Horses" in 2019. Meg edited and co-authored a third title in 2022, a world first, international collaboration of authors. This international collaboration is titled "Nourished: Horses, Animals & Nature in Counselling, Psychotherapy & Mental Health". These ground-breaking books received praise and endorsement from academics and leading professionals in the field, across the nation and around the globe, for their engaging and in-depth look inside the inner workings of equine, animal and nature assisted practice.

When Meg is not training students from across the globe in equine, animal, and nature assisted psychotherapy, and I-Thou Inter-species Relating, she spends her time caring for thirteen family herd members, eight kangaroo friends, three expressive cats, and dear dog, Bear, who is never far from her side. Never forgetting her loving husband, Noel, and two beautiful daughters, Rose and Jasmine. Meg lives and breathes the wisdom of animals and nature. It is her Life's Work to be an aware and loving mother and animal-carer, and a quiet warrior, seeking to make the world a safer place for horses, animals and people through her practice and teachings.

CONTENTS

About the Author VII
Beginnings 15
The First Commitment: Love 25
The Second Commitment: Values 47
The Third Commitment: Personal Development 55
The Fourth Commitment: Trauma-Informed 71
The Fifth Commitment: Phenomenology 85
The Sixth Commitment: Science 95
The Seventh Commitment: Practice & Discipline 123
The Eighth Commitment: Ethics & Enrichment 153
The Journey Ahead 159
References 163

HORSES, LOVE & SCIENCE

BEGINNINGS

> THIS BOOK IS DESIGNED FOR YOU, THE EVERY-DAY, LOVING, HORSEPERSON WHO WANTS TO DO THE ABSOLUTE BEST FOR THEIR HORSES AND LEARN A FRAMEWORK FOR DEEPENING THE RELATIONSHIP AND INTERSPECIES CONNECTION YOU SHARE.

I hope this book is supportive for the every-day horse-person and the equine assisted practice students and practitioners, including those of you learning our EPI model (The Equine Psychotherapy Institute) and other approaches of equine assisted psychotherapy, equine facilitated psychotherapy, equine assisted learning, equine facilitated learning around the world.

My journey toward a life with horses has been anything but traditional. Far from the young girl yearning for a pony and growing up with the gift of riding lessons and equine companions, it wasn't until I reached 30 that horses changed my life, firstly in the form of a chestnut gelding named Mav. Mav was a 16 hand high former racehorse who was not a sensible choice for a beginner but was kind and calm enough to tolerate me. Mav not only opened my home to many more equine friendships in the years to follow, but he opened my mind and my heart too. He introduced me to the way of the horse (equine nature and behaviour) and taught me many lessons in becoming more aware, more grounded, more courageous, and caring. Some of those lessons were beautiful and some were terrifying, but all the lessons were invaluable. I wish I could repay the gift he gave me, and meet him again now, as a more aware, I-Thou horse person. I pay respects to Mav in every moment I am kind, clear and intentional with each and every horse I encounter today.

I am comfortable to admit that I'm not an expert horse person, horse trainer and I am not a particularly good rider. My temperament and personal qualities include heightened sensitivity, wilfulness, intense feelings, and emotions. I like change, unpredictability, freedom, and creativity. Many excellent horse men, women and animal trainers I have met or read about are consistent, calm, and even-tempered. They enjoy and display tendencies for consistency, predictability, sameness, and discipline. These tendencies are a good fit for relating with horses and horse training (and animal training) in general, but are not my natural talents per se. I had to develop these characteristics and capacities over time.

Over the last two and a half decades of living and learning with horses (and other species), I've had to work hard on, and work around, my genetics, temperament and tendencies, including my busy career as a psychotherapist and my training responsibilities (in my role as an equine, animal and nature assisted psychotherapy trainer). Not forgetting my full life as a dedicated mother of two gorgeous, sensitive, talented, non-horsey, but animal-obsessed daughters (who are now 18 and 23 years of age).

My passion for horses and all animals has kept me growing and learning throughout all of my life, particularly over the last 24 years, even though my progress as a horse trainer has been slow. My approach with horses has crystallised over the last 12 years into a clear system of relating. I teach this system of relating with horses as the foundation of my Equine Assisted Psychotherapy and Equine Assisted Learning training programs at The Equine Psychotherapy Institute (EPI). I teach an adapted version of this approach with animals of different species as I-Thou Interspecies Relating too. When students have asked me for literature to support their learning journey toward understanding and applying I-Thou Horsepersonship, I have mainly used the spoken word, various articles, videos and presentations to teach the approach.

Seemingly, in line with my journey toward a life with horses, I thought, "It's better late than never!" (as those who know me understand, I am often late!). So here is the overdue book on my brainchild 'I-Thou Horsepersonship'. The term and the words are a mouthful, but I am not comfortable with Horsemanship or Horse Training, as neither are correct or inclusive enough to convey my approach. I founded this approach and have taught it to my students from 2011 until this current day. I intend to be teaching it for a long time, as it feels to be one of the most meaningful parts of my Life's Work.

The I-Thou Horsepersonship approach was introduced to the public in my first book, *An Introduction to Equine Assisted Psychotherapy: principles, theory and practice of the Equine Psychotherapy Institute Model* (2016). I further shared the approach through a combination of education support materials such as articles in training manuals, our online equine studies portal, lectures and conference presentations (from conferences both at our institute (EPI Conference) in 2018, and at the HERD Institute Conference in 2019). In 2022, I introduced the ethical orientation of I-Thou Horsepersonship in the chapter titled *For the Love of Horses* in the book I edited and co-authored *Nourished: Horses, Animals and Nature in Counselling, Psychotherapy and Mental Health*. This book showcased international education experts from around the world working with equine assisted therapy, animal assisted therapy and nature assisted therapy. It appears that many students and practitioners around the world utilise my I-Thou Horsepersonship approach, however this book is my first attempt at documenting and operationalising the I-Thou Horsepersonship approach in full.

My goal is to operationalise this way of being with horses, training horses, learning with horses and learning from horses, as simply as I can. It is a kind, loving, safe and simple approach, where horses have their species-specific needs met, and where horses benefit from the relationship with people. This has always been a central feature of my personal mission and the Institute's mission: to improve the quality of life, wellbeing and *lived subjective experience* of all horses living with people. As I said earlier, this approach with horses, and all animals, is an important part of my Life's Work.

In the past, and too often still in the present day, many horses endure loss, violation, and punishment due to ignorance, misunderstanding and unintentional harm produced by unaware people and horse-human relationships, as well as non-reflective traditions or standards of horse care and horse training.

When interacting with horses or considering a particular training approach or method, a good rule of thumb I share with people, is to ask yourself the following questions:

1. Would I feel comfortable or okay doing *this* (insert any interaction with horse) with my other (human and non-human) friends, family or loved ones?
2. If I did *this* (or a parallel of this request, amount of pressure, demand or specific behaviour) with a friend, family member, colleague, student, neighbour or animal friend

    ...would they want to spend time with me?

    ...would they feel safe with me?

    ...would they feel my care?

    ...would they understand my communications?

    ...would they feel some mutual benefit or enjoyment?

    ...would they feel an ability to express, say yes, or no?

    ...would they feel enriched in some way?

    ...would they feel loved?

If not, it might be time to reflect, pause and try something different.

Be kind to yourself as you learn about I-Thou Horsepersonship. Be kind to your horses.

I hope to give some practical ideas to support your Care, Open Curiosity, and Creativity as a horse person.

I believe that all our interactions and relationships (including learning and teaching-based relating) must be governed by basic ethics and non-harming values, as a minimum. Given that we now know human and non-human social mammals all have feelings and emotions, experience fear, pain and suffering and have brains that are socially wired (Bekoff, 2000); it is our responsibility to ensure anyone in our care is treated ethically and has the opportunity to experience a

good quality of life, dictated by their species-specific needs (Masson & McCarthy, 1995). I don't believe an anthropocentric (human-centred) perspective is ethical and it can never be truly safe, in the context of inter-species relating. Awareness, phenomenology, insight, reflection and education are together, the archenemy of the unconscious, anthropocentric perspective. It is a serious responsibility to care for others (including other children, adults and non-human social mammals in our care). I believe it is our shared responsibility to ensure *we are all* emotionally, psychologically and physically safe, healthy and well.

Owning, living with and learning with horses is a privilege that brings significant responsibilities. Responsibilities require commitments. Let's deep dive into the eight commitments of I-Thou Horsepersonship.

THE 8 COMMITMENTS AND RESPONSIBILITIES OF I-THOU HORSEPERSONSHIP

1. LOVE

2. VALUES

3. PERSONAL DEVELOPMENT

4. TRAUMA-INFORMED

5. PHENOMENOLOGY

6. SCIENCE

7. PRACTICE & DISCIPLINE

8. ETHICS & ENRICHMENT

THE 8 COMMITMENTS OF I-THOU HORSEPERSONSHIP

LOVE
Demonstrate your Love daily through your I-Thou skills
in Presence, Inclusion, Confirmation and Commitment to Dialogue.

VALUES
Be intentional, explicit and expressive of your Values in Relationship,
holding yourself accountable in every meeting together.

PERSONAL DEVELOPMENT
Know Yourself. Your nervous state, sensations, feelings, thoughts,
behaviours, your belief and relationship patterns or tendencies,
as you impact, relate and create safe relationship.

TRAUMA-INFORMED
Seek to understand your horses' expressions of trauma. Track your
horses' signals of relaxation, interest, seeking, stress, pain and
traumatised states. Use your Support Toolkit.

PHENOMENOLOGY
Notice 'What is'. Track your Horses' subjective experience as expressed
through their energy, body language, orienting and behaviour.

SCIENCE
Know and intelligently integrate current equine science and equitation science
principles and practices in your everyday relating with horses.

PRACTICE & DISCIPLINE
Take regular Herd Sits, offer Pleasure-oriented Touch, use your
I-Thou in the Approach, Halter and Requests, take Walks
Together and include Aware Riding, if you ride.

ETHICS & ENRICHMENT
Focus on what is safe and good for your horse. Focus on what enriches
the horse-human-natural environment system. We are all Nature.

HORSES, LOVE & SCIENCE

THE FIRST COMMITMENT: LOVE

A New Perspective

A lot of people I meet who see themselves as 'horsey' would openly say they love horses. They might say, "I'm a horse lover" or, "I'm in love with horses." What I've noticed, however, is that everyone has a very different meaning, understanding and description of *what love is*, and what *love for the horse* looks like.

In this chapter I want to do the very difficult work, from my perspective, of operationalising what I mean by a love-focused approach with horses or love-focused horse training. To do this I am going to introduce you to Martin Buber's principles of I-Thou relating and to psychotherapy (Buber, 1923). Surprisingly, there are many parallels between being a *psychotherapist* who supports change, growth and learning with a human and being a *horse person* or *horse trainer*, who supports change, growth and learning with horses. *Both are supporting learning, growth and change in the Other and working directly with the mechanism of change, in the context of relationship.* The psychotherapist works in the human-to-human context, which may or may not include dysfunction, trauma or challenges experienced by the *human client*. The horse person or horse trainer, works in the horse-human context, supporting learning in the horse, and fostering a safe inter-species relationship between horse and human, where the horse recipient may or may not have a broader historic context of difficulty or trauma (in captivity with humans). I-Thou relating, I believe, is paramount for both. Let me try to explain why.

I learned about I-Thou relating and what is also referred to as 'dialogic relating' during my psychotherapy training 25 years ago whilst studying psychotherapy and learning to become a psychotherapist, specifically, a Gestalt psychotherapist, across a three-year diploma program. I studied psychotherapy after first completing a degree majoring in both Psychology and Sociology, a Masters in Social Work, followed by specialist training in Developmental Psychiatry.

Gestalt Therapy was founded by Fritz and Laura Perls in the 1940s and 1950s and is a humanistic and awareness-based approach that focuses on a client's immediate experience in the Here and Now, in relationship. Gestalt Therapy has a developmental and field theoretical lens, understanding that all behavioural, emotional and cognitive patterns have intelligent origins in earlier life experience, contextualised in the environment, system or field the human being developed in. Gestalt Therapy is an inherently creative practice. At its heart, it is an experiential, experimental and relational approach. This too is the basis of good horsepersonship – being experiential, experimental and relational.

In Australia, relationally-oriented Gestalt Psychotherapy training is now a four year program, but what hasn't changed is the fundamental teachings in I-Thou relating utilising Martin Buber's principles and practices. I-Thou relating principles are used to guide and teach the therapist how to *fully listen to* and *feel into* the perspective of the client and learn to be in a relationship in a way that is present, patient, intentional and committed, and that intends to meet the deeper development and psychological needs of the client. All human clients, it is believed, have core needs to feel heard, seen, and valued in their individuality and for their *unique being and humanity*. This relational perspective and therapeutic relationship was not taught in the university psychology, social work and developmental psychiatry education and studies I engaged in, so it was not until I trained in Gestalt psychotherapy that I learned more (academically and experientially) about the significant relational and therapeutic practice of I-Thou relating.

I-Thou relating felt to me to be such an incredibly rich source of being *present* to another person, and to another being, in a way where there was clarity, focus, intentionality and a desire to deeply understand the subjective experience of *the other*, to get as close to *being inside somebody else's perspective, inside somebody else's skin, feelings and being, including* their needs, wants, motivations and individuality, as possible. So, it allows us to *intentionally* get as close as humanly possible to 'the other,' despite the constraints of (obviously) *not being the other*. This brings challenges with human-to-human relating, and of course, brings challenges in inter-species relating with non-human mammals. Challenges, I believe, that are deeply rewarding for all parties involved.

I liked this way of relating, as it added a lot of clarity to the relationship and the goal of the relating, namely – **being with the other for no other purpose than to deeply know, feel, and understand the other's uniqueness and be open to the meeting together in the present moment.** This actually mirrors the main qualities of the Good Enough Parent or the Good Enough mother, father, parent or caregiver of the infant or child. The Good Enough Parent wishes to understand, and listen deeply to their infant, to get to know their child, to be attuned to their child's nervous system, body, feelings and needs, including the child's unique ways of perceiving, relating and behaving.

Therefore, I believe that in many ways, this I-Thou method of relating operationalises the essential qualities of love. Love includes listening deeply to the other, seeing the other for who they are, valuing the other, accepting the other unconditionally as they are, committing to working through misunderstandings, struggles, difficulties, conflict or differences from a perspective of integrity, honesty, and intentionality. It is the capacity to take in the other with a deep knowing that their value and their essentially unique being has inherent beauty and value, regardless of their expression, communication, or behaviour in the present moment. Love includes a degree of unconditional positive regard, deep acceptance, and care. The togetherness, bond and attachment experience go well beyond trying to influence, shape or change the other, into a world of being-together and presence.

Hopefully, as you read about I-Thou relating in the psychotherapy context, you are starting to draw some parallels to the horsepersonship context of horse-human relating and horse training.

I-Thou Theory

The terms *I-Thou relating* and *dialogic relating* (in the literature) are used interchangeably. When the word dialogic is used, it is not referring to speech, but rather an attitude, an awareness, an openness and a caring about the unique other and the interconnectedness.

Rich Hycner (1995) refers to dialogic relating in a nutshell as an attitude of genuinely feeling, sensing and experiencing the other person, as a person, not an object or a part object. It includes a willingness to deeply hear and feel the other person's experience without prejudgment, assumption, or interpretation. It includes a willingness to simply connect.

When we understand I-Thou relating or dialogic relating as both an attitude, capacity or skill, we can start to see the direct applicability of I-Thou relating in the context of interspecies interactions, where the predominant dialogue is non-verbal. For example, in horse-human interactions the dialogic relating is based on body language, posture, orienting, nervous state, and behaviours, (including the context of attachment history and lived experience).

In the 1960s Laura Perls, the wife of Fritz Perls discussed the unfortunate tendency for Gestalt therapy to be misunderstood as a *demonstration method* that was more *technique based* (technical), rather than *relationally based*. This was unfortunate as it unintentionally promoted an incorrect and simplified view of gestalt therapy as technique-focused and non-relational. This could not be further from the truth in contemporary gestalt psychotherapy.

Laura believed that a Gestalt Therapist *does not use techniques*, rather the therapist is inherently *relationship focused*. Many psychotherapies tend to focus on *technique*, to the detriment of the client's prognosis. Research suggests that client prognosis is in fact shaped by *the client's experience of the therapeutic relationship*, their experience of the therapist, and the placebo effect (Cozolino, 2017). The placebo effect is not a random positive effect of the mind of the recipient, rather, it is a result of the relational and attachment experience and the social brain of the client, which is working at the level of oxytocin, dopamine and other chemicals being released in the context of safe and pleasurable relating and relationships.

This issue highlights the difference, strengths and limitations of what you could broadly think of as '*technique focused change makers*' and '*relationally (and social brain) oriented change makers*'.

I believe the above issues highlight some interesting parallels for horsepersonship and horse training. Specifically, horse people who focus purely on strategic, technique-focused and behavioural learning approaches will miss the growth, change and learning that can happen at the relational level of the social brain of the horse, including the nervous state, feelings, attachment, and relationship level.

Both the human mammal and equine mammal are social mammals, have social brains, attachment tendencies and needs, and are fundamentally *relationally wired* in order to grow, thrive and survive. Therefore, it stands to reason that certain attachment and environmental needs must be met for both the healthy human and healthy horse *individuals* to learn and grow (despite all the other significant differences between the equine and human characteristics and species). Technique-oriented, behaviourally oriented horse trainers, or horse people who objectify the horse, use positive punishment methods (unconsciously or intentionally) or other unaware, ad hoc training methods *risk missing a horse's relational needs for a safe, regulated 'other', who is present (in touch with reality and observant), attuned and responsive* to the nervous state, arousal, feelings or emotional state, and unique tendencies of the horse, in the present moment.

It is the proposition of I-Thou Horsepersonship that to support safe change and learning in the 'whole horse' we must include both relationally-oriented and technique-based approaches in our horsepersonship and horse training. We include science and behavioural approaches, including specialised learning theory applications such as classical conditioning, habituation and desensitisation, and a combination of reinforcement techniques, alongside a *relationally-oriented container and commitment to* love, clear values, personal development, trauma-informed understanding, phenomenology, practice and discipline, as well as ethics and enrichment.

In the psychotherapy context, we use the human-meeting-human relationship to produce change. In the horse training context, we aim to produce change related to learning outcomes (e.g., in the context of equitation, riding or performance of the ridden horse), and growth, shared learning and bonding, through the horse and human relationship. When we are in relationship with horses, or in the context of horse human interactions, we're not only working with the human-defined educational or training needs, we're often also supporting learning in a horse, who may have varying degrees of trauma, stress and nervous state function. A horse's learning and functioning is also influenced by the horse's genetics, temperament and history, which includes attachment with their mother and natal herd environment, as well as the human interaction they have been exposed to. Prior interactions with humans may have been stressful and produced trauma responses or they may have supported the horse's secure attachment and produced calm responses. These early interactions may include veterinary treatment, dentistry, hoof trimming, weaning, initial handling and groundwork, ridden experiences and much more.

In some ways, this parallels the situation psychotherapists find themselves in in the context of the therapeutic room (or setting). The clinician or therapist might find themselves working with a client who has a secure attachment and robust sense of self, who is working to learn about particular aspects of themselves or make changes in their lives. Or the therapist might be working with someone with significant complex trauma, post-traumatic stress disorder, or other enduring psychological disorders or psychiatric disorders and attachment disorders dictated by the client's attachment history, early life experience, developing brain, temperament, family, social and broader systemic environment and inter-sectional factors co-shaping the client's current functioning.

The I-Thou Horsepersonship approach believes that we can only foster solid growth and change by *being in relationship with the whole horse*, not just the behaviour of the horse, or one isolated aspect of the horse, for example, their movement, biomechanics, or behaviour, only.

So how do we become relationally-oriented horse-people?

Let us turn our minds back to Martin Buber. He purported that genuine dialogic relating or I-Thou relating (which remember is non-verbal) requires a regard for the Other as the very One she or he is, in their difference, and uniqueness. It requires an acceptance, fully, of the Other as they are. In the context of horse training and horsepersonship, if we understand and apply the I-Thou principles it requires that the chief focus of the horse person is *relating with horse in the here and now (as they are)*, including a regard for the horse as the very *unique individual* they are! So, the I-Thou Horse Person (I-Thou HP) is aware of the horse's inherently different characteristics, nature, including the species-specific ways she or he responds, behaves, moves, feels, orients and needs. The I-Thou HP sees, values and accepts the horse fully, in every approach, meeting, moment of relating, request, communication or interaction. Every communication from the I-Thou HP is influenced by the individual horse, in the present moment. The I-Thou HP brings their *whole being* to meet the whole *otherness* (of the horse) in every encounter. This degree of presence, of being to being relating, is uncommon, and is life changing (certainly for the human!)

The basic tenant of a relationally oriented psychotherapy, like Gestalt therapy, is that the overall psychotherapy approach is that *the process and the goal is relational or dialogic in nature*. Any techniques used, arrive only *out of the context of relationship between the client and the therapist in the present moment*. It is the dialogue or the attention to 'the between' that becomes the focus, not the techniques or goals per se. It is a way of being, and philosophical approach (values, ethics and relationally dictated). It honours the truth about all social mammals - in the beginning, there is only relationship. There is no such thing as an *individual* or separate human, separate from the human family, tribe or society. There is no individual horse, separate from the herd and evolution of the equine species.

So, change must be fundamentally understood from a relational lens, a lens that includes the relational needs of the whole horse, and the whole human.

There is no I, without a Thou (I and Thou) or an It (I and It). So, what then is I-Thou and I-It, and how does it look in horsepersonship or horse training?

I Thou Relating – Presence-based relating

The I-Thou experience then in the psychotherapy context is one where the therapist is being as *fully present* as one can be, to the client, with little self-centred purpose or goal in mind. It's an experience of appreciating the otherness or the uniqueness and the wholeness of the other, the client, in their humanity and human uniqueness.

I-It Relating – Strategic-relating

I-It relating, in contrast, is thoroughly purposeful. There is a goal in mind and there is a subservience of the personhood or the whole person of the other, in order to focus on the goal. Techniques are used to achieve a goal for change in the other. So, it requires objectifying the other and it is a strategic form of relating. A by-product of focusing on the goal, means the *whole person* inevitably becomes secondary to the behavioural outcome to be achieved. An I-It is attitude is not inherently wrong or bad. In fact, it's a part of relating. It is only concerning in the psychotherapy context when it becomes one's overwhelmingly predominant way of relating, or when the client feels the therapist is not attuned, present, or understanding their perspective or experience.

In our modern and busy, task-focused world, many people feel objectified, missed, and devalued, in transactional exchanges and interactions focused on achievement and behavioural change or outcomes. I-It becomes problematic when it's predominant in any relationship, but certainly in the context of a therapeutic relationship. If this objectifying attitude is out of balance with a dialogic approach or I-Thou relating, people can feel missed, misunderstood and just 'a number' or 'client.'

I-It Horsepersonship

So, in a horse training or horsepersonship context, the I-It stance is the technique focused, strategically-focused horse person intent only on producing a change of behaviour in the horse, to meet the needs of the person. The whole-horse-experience and *subjective experience* of the horse becomes subservient to the goal, which is to change the horse's behaviour, and produce a response in alignment with the learning goals, the person's goals. So, the horse in this moment must become objectified. When this attitude becomes the predominant way of relating, the horse can be missed (the horse's nervous state, emotions, wants, tendencies and needs become irrelevant), and the horse-human relating, bond and attachment too can be missed. In this situation, the *potential* of the horse will be missed, as of course will the creative potential of the horse-human relationship. At worst, the horse's social needs, emotional needs, and attachment needs are neglected, violated, abused or punished. Sometimes this happens even with the very best intentions, sometimes not.

LOVE AND I-THOU

The I-Thou approach gets as close to defining love as anything else I have learned, read, thought about or been exposed to! Many people describe love as an intense feeling of deep affection or deep attachment. Others describe the intentionality and commitment-focused aspects of love, over the long term. Either way, I believe the four qualities and capacities of the I-Thou relationship really capture much of what I define as love.

Let's explore the four qualities and attitudes of the I-Thou approach, which I refer to as - *The Love Focused Approach*.

The first quality and attitude is *Presence*, which is an open, aware, mindful and embodied being.

The second quality and attitude is *Inclusion*, which is a deep, empathic, and attuned responsiveness.

The third quality and attitude is *Commitment to Dialogue* (non-verbal dialogue) which is relating with commitment and enduring challenge and difficulty in relationship.

The fourth quality and attitude is *Confirmation* which is unconditional acceptance, valuing and honouring the other and the potential of the other at all times.

Let's further discuss these four capacities that you need to develop, to practice love-focused horse relating, horse education or horsepersonship.

1. Presence: Being *ALL THERE* with your Horse – being aware, mindful and embodied

Let's operationalise presence in a sensible, easy to understand way. You can think of presence as I am here.

I am here.

I am grounded.

I'm aware.

I am embodied.

I'm in the present moment.

I'm connected to my senses.

I can see hear, smell, taste, touch.

I'm aware in the present moment and I'm here with You.

Sounds easy, but it is not! Most people are in fact not aware, present, and embodied. It takes a lot of practice to move out of 'automatic pilot,' out of a dominant thinking-based way of relating, including reflection, strategising, planning, judging, theorising, getting attached to my ideas, opinions, thoughts, wants, needs etc.

When I am present, I am NOT, stuck in my thoughts, my agenda, my tense body, or my frightened sensations, my 'pretending to be confident' behaviour, hijacked by my ideas of being a 'horse person' or 'horse trainer' or attached to the *role* I play when I am with my horse. Being 'in role' requires an artificial *seeming*, trying, or pretending to be in a certain way, that is essentially not my authentic experience or authentic, experiential truth in the present moment. Being in role demands that I am not fully present.

When I am present, I am NOT fixed in a forceful, controlling, demanding, patterned way of behaving. I am NOT disassociated, away in the clouds, dancing in fanciful ideas, lofty dreams and imaginative poems about horses as magical, spiritual, unicorn creatures or dreaming of or expecting the horse to be my healer.

THE FIRST COMMITMENT: LOVE

PRESENCE SUPPORT EXERCISE:
OUTBREATH AND GROUNDING

1. Use your outbreath or your let down breath, just as horses do, to let go of any excess tension or energy in the body right now. Take an outbreath. It might be a slow, soft outbreath, or it might be a big snort outbreath like the horses do. Take an outbreath to help you arrive. Next ground yourself. Bring your awareness to your feet on the ground, tuning into everything that you can sense in the contact between your feet and the earth. Right now. What are you noticing in the contact between your body and your feet and the earth? The ground and the earth below? Does it feel light or solid or heavy or stable or balanced or unbalanced? Are there particular sensations that you can feel through the contact that are solid, or moving, or pulsating, or vibrating? Just take a moment to really tune into that contact between yourself your feet and the earth. Bring your attention down through your body all the way to the feet to the earth.

2. Use your outbreath and your grounding to support you to become Present. This is both a regulation exercise and support *and* an awareness exercise and support. So, you may notice you start to feel a little calmer, settled and stable inside (regulated nervous state) and you may notice that you start to perceive things a little more clearly. Your senses may start to feel a bit more heightened, crisp or vibrant (greater awareness of the field). So, you may experience a shift in your awareness of the field or the environment, the others (any others or other beings you are in proximity to), and to yourself—your self-awareness may start to increase, and you may be able to start to notice more of your breath, body sensations, feelings, thoughts. This is the presence you need to bring every time you approach and meet your horses. Practice these exercises every day, and before you approach and meet your horses.

*I am in my body, my self-experience,
in touch with reality (in this present moment,
in this specific moment, context and
environment), grounded and right 'here'.*

2. Inclusion: Being With Your Own <u>and</u> Your Horses Subjective Experience, at the Same Time – using empathic attunement alongside self-awareness

This skill and attitude of inclusion, as the word suggests, includes *your experience* and the *other's experience*. Developing skills to bring an *intentional and dedicated interest in the other's* nervous system and state (arousal levels, stress, activation-deactivation cycles, regulation, dysregulation); in the other's body (posture, tightness, looseness, body language, signs and communications, biomechanics, movement and way of moving); in the other's feelings and emotional range; in the other's orientating responses and behaviours; and in their perspective or umwelt, way of relating and being, whilst being connected to and informed by your own experience. You are fascinated in the other's subjective experience in relationship with you, and your self-experience in relationship, and their self-experience in general! This intentionality takes you into the edges of feeling, thinking and imagining what would it be like (from experiential lens) to *be* this unique other being, to *be* this *horse* before you? As mentioned, inclusion includes *your own experience in the present moment,* so it includes your presence and your experience, as you are shuttling into, or bringing your attention to your *horse's experience and your own experience in the co-created* experience (as you are impacting each other and co-shaping each-others experience in the interacting).

The open curiosity you bring in inclusion feels soft and spacious, and includes feeling into:

Who are you today, Horse?

How are you feeling?

What are you experiencing right now?

What are you wanting?

Where is your attention?

What are you doing?

What is your perspective?

What is your perception?

Presence allows and supports me to be Here - I (Human) am Here

    Inclusivity allows the *horse to arrive to you!* – You (Horse) are Here

    So now we have two vital elements or ingredients for love-focused relating, which are *'I am fully Here'* and now *'**you are Here'*** to me, with me, as we relate or interact together.

EXERCISE:
BE WITH YOUR HORSE

Sit or stand comfortably and safely in front of your horse, using your outbreath and grounding skills (from previous exercise) to support your presence.

When you feel present to your horse say, "I am here."

Focus on your horse, whilst still remaining in a state of presence.

When you feel present to truly seeing your horse say, "You are here."

3. Commitment to Dialogue: I will not give up on You or on 'Us'.

This principle and attitude towards horses includes the commitment to take full responsibility, to be a dedicated horse owner and horse-friend, the same kind of dedication that you offer any other of your dear friends and family.

"I'm here to be with you, to learn from you, to learn in relationship with you for the rest of our lives, together."

This brings a big shift to move away from a conditional way of relating with horses. For example, if you behave in this way, I will keep you, I will enjoy you or be with you. If you behave that way, I will judge you, give up on you, sell you or rehome you. So, this is a really challenging attitude and practice, where the horse owner commits to a life of learning in relationship, through relationship with this unique other - the horse.

This commitment requires hard work.

It's hard work to be in relationship. It's hard work to be in any long-term relationship. Anyone in a long-term, intentional and aware human to human relationship understands that it's hard work. It's not easy for two unique beings, two individuals with their different temperaments, their different patterns, their different ways of perceiving, their different perspectives, their different behaviours, their different histories, to get along, to live together, to understand each other, to communicate, to be in relationship, with kindness and growth. This principle requires commitment and discipline around not giving up, working with and through differences and conflict, as a matter of course, as a part of healthy relationships.

This does not mean enduring something that is harmful or unsafe. What it does mean is that the relationship, and the value of the relationship is primarily in the service of mutual benefit, growth and learning, learning from the other, learning with the other, and growing through the relationship and the lived experience, including the difficulties. So, this practice includes bringing in care, patience and creativity to work with ruptures and repair. It focuses on a deeper understanding of *what is needed to co-exist and communicate*, and an ongoing commitment to finding safe ways to be together, to learn together, to grow together, and to be in relationship. This principle dictates that every difference, every difficulty, every rupture, every misunderstanding between horse and person is an opportunity to learn and an opportunity to grow. It is an opportunity to deepen the relationship, through understanding, acceptance of difference, and finding *creative ways* to communicate, adjust, manage, repair and thrive together.

Horse-human relating is particularly challenging, due to the differences across the species. Now, in some ways, our herd tendencies are similar to those of horses and our play tendencies are similar to horses in some ways too. However, people still misunderstand and have unrealistic expectations of their horse's tendency to prefer the company of their herd or pair bond, and misunderstand the horse's natural tendencies around seeking, curiosity, exploring the environment with their body, mouth, and teeth. The horse's prey tendencies are very challenging for a lot of people to have a clear cognitive understanding of and to show an experientially-based deep appreciation and empathic attunement toward. Many horse people appear to get triggered by a horse's prey tendencies, such as becoming fearful and frightened, sometimes very suddenly (as with shies). People can regress into *name-calling* (e.g., calling the horse "stupid" or "naughty" or "manipulative"), *anthropomorphising* (e.g., "Oh, the horse is doing this deliberately to get out of work"), and resorting to *anxious controlling tendencies, uncontrolled punishment, and violence* if they (the person) become frightened, frustrated, angry or overwhelmed and unsure of what to do.

Horse people have an ethical responsibility to have an understanding of equine science and basic horse behaviour, perception, communications, and needs. But on top of this, the I-Thou Horseperson also commits to being in inter-species dialogue, for the long haul! This means understanding that, as in all healthy long-term relationships, working with and through difficulties and differences (alongside the moments of ease, joy and harmony) is the true work of relationship.

This journey is what all long-term relationships are about, not the destination! So, the I-Thou Horseperson brings the disciplined attitude of "I am here to be with you, to learn with you, to grow with you, to understand your species-specific needs and individuality, and to find safe ways to grow together in relationship."

The relationship is the destination.

EXERCISE:
DEVELOP A PLEDGE OR COMMITMENT STATEMENT TO YOUR HORSE

Create a simple statement that you can stick to your fridge with a magnet that outlines your commitment to your horse.

"[Insert Your Horse's Name], my truest desire is to always see your essential equine nature, meet your species-specific needs, and find safe, and mutually enriching ways to be together, to learn together, and grow. I pledge my commitment to you and our relationship."

4. Confirmation – Unconditional acceptance

Confirmation requires an attitude of valuing the horse's uniqueness and absolute essential worth, regardless of whether you like or dislike their confirmation, colour, behaviour, tendencies, feelings or expression. It is an understanding that sits deep within us, knowing that each unique being on earth, by their very birthright deserves and has the right to be viewed as a valuable being. So, confirmation includes an attitude toward your horse of, "I see you and I value you."

I find this attitude and practice essential for all people, but particularly for horse people and riders who make complex requests of horses on the ground or under saddle and can get caught up in confusing the horse's behaviour with their worth.

In healthy parenting and relationship work, it is well known that it is important to communicate to the other, a separation of the *behaviour* from the *being*. For example, in the context of a parent-child communication, "That behaviour is not OK," as opposed to, "You are not OK." As an extension of this confirmation attitude and practice in the broader context with horses, when you add in the human's performance wants, attachment to results, looks, achievements, status desires etc., there is an even greater need for the practice of confirmation and deep appreciation for the other, as well as an understanding of their potential to grow and actualise (under fertile conditions). The welfare and safety of the horse are fundamentally dependent on the human's capacity to have values, to have a strong moral compass and ethical approach that is all glued together by confirmation capacities and commitment.

Otherwise, training horses and being with horses can essentially become a "use" of the horse for the human's pleasure, achievement, performance, status, desires or healing.

It is human nature that we can sometimes become preoccupied with our own perspective and sometimes this can cloud our perception and perspective in relationship with human friends and family, as well as non-human friends and family.

Our horses need ultimately to be seen, to be heard, to be valued to be accepted and cared for in a way that is over and above your human desires for enjoyment, pleasure, or performance outcomes. Horses must be seen for the equine species that they are, fundamentally different to the human species (even with some shared social mammal characteristics). The individual horse or horses each horseperson spends time with or trains, is uniquely different to any other horse alive on the planet. Only when we value the inherent worth of each horse, and inherent uniqueness of each horse, can we build mutually beneficial, nourishing and safe relationships (alongside training goals) with our horses.

EXERCISE:
SIT AND OBSERVE THE HORSES' ESSENTIAL BEING AND INHERENT VALUE WITH NO AGENDA

Spend 30 minutes to sit with your horse or herd, in a position that allows the horses to continue grazing, resting or relating as they are. Use your outbreath, grounding and then focus on your Senses - what you can smell, hear, touch and see. From this place, begin to observe your horses with *soft eyes*, as they interact naturally with their environment. Hold this appreciation in mind,

"I see you. I honour your inherent value, worth and uniqueness."

In my book *Nourished: Horses, Animals and Nature in Counselling, Psychotherapy and Mental Health*, published in 2022, I describe the difference between I-Thou relating and I-It relating. In the chapter, I overview I-It relating as "strategic relating". As mentioned, I-It is not in itself bad or wrong, in fact it's helpful sometimes and is a natural part of human relating. I-It only becomes a problem when people get fixed in this way of relating, and are unaware of this or are unable to orient to others in an I-Thou relationship. When we focus on others predominantly in an I-It manner, it means I am relating to you, for the purpose of changing you, manipulating you, reflecting on you, objectifying you, wishing to influence and use you in order to achieve something. Essentially, you then become an extension of my wants, desires or needs. It is strategic in nature. We function in an I-It manner when we have goals that we want to achieve, so my relating with you has the purpose of 'achievement of goal fulfilment' as the predominant stance.

I-It relating is common in the horse world, where the human relates to the horse from the perspective (unconsciously or without awareness) of prioritising their own goals, pleasure, performance outcomes or feelings *over* their horse's tendencies, subjective experience, species-specific needs and true mutuality in relationship. The *care* or *love* that the fixed I-It person offers, is through eyes that demand anthropomorphising, an anthropocentric view and projection. Here, I am projecting my experience, thoughts, needs and wants onto the Other, without awareness of doing so. Hence, it is not a seeing that comes from observing the equine for who they essentially are (in their species-specific tendencies and uniqueness).

Some examples of I-It care and anthropomorphic 'love' comments might include:

Oh, he loves being stabled.

He loves his three doona rugs.

She loves dressage.

This horse is born to race, he loves winning.

My horse absolutely hates all other horses, he thinks he's a person (or a dog).

She's a pretty paddock ornament.

He's completely bombproof.

My horse is cuddly, like a teddy bear.

She loves me so much. She knows exactly how to make me feel better.

My horse is an amazing therapist, he knows what to do to make me feel better.

He loves healing my clients, he knows when they are coming, and exactly what to do.

THE FIRST COMMITMENT: LOVE

Some examples of I-It care and anthropocentric actions might include:

Stabling horses for human convenience.

Medicating or feeding horses for performance over wellbeing.

Separation of Horses for human needs.

Individual yards and paddocks for human convenience and access.

People fixed in projective patterns and anthropomorphising tendencies are not generally aware of this distorted perception and relating tendency and are often surprised when they start to learn about and notice it. When they begin to 'peel back' the layers of their own thoughts and beliefs (that have been sitting in the background, unintentionally motivating and shaping their perception and behaviour) they can become clearer about where they learned this thinking, and why they do what they do. These thoughts and beliefs are sometimes closely tied to a person's sense of self and self-identity. Often people unintentionally do the same (projecting) with their children, partners, friends, and other animals. It is a common human way of relating, rather than uncommon. *Only personal development work and new knowledge can start to bring these tendencies to light.* In our Institute training, more often than not, it is a shock for students to start to have a look at all the ways they have been projecting, objectifying, using and strategically relating with their horses, that on the surface appear light or funny, but underneath, can be deeply meaningful and can say a lot about the personal history, tendencies, functioning, patterns and unmet needs as a younger person or adult.

In summary, I-Thou Horsepersonship requires presence, inclusivity, confirmation, and commitment to dialogue. It intentionally brings the subjective experience of the horse, the needs of the horse and the mutuality between the horse and the human into more of a *balanced position*.

When you think of the relationships in your life that include other species or other people, where love is the primary orienting ingredient, you will find shared listening. You may also find a desire to feel into the other's world, perspective, wants and needs, a desire to offer an attuned responsiveness, a deep valuing of the other's uniqueness and individuality, a unconditional acceptance and a commitment to learning and growing together. So, too for the I-Thou Horse Person.

I believe that if you practice the four skills and capacities of presence, inclusion, confirmation and commitment to dialogue each and every time you approach and spend time with your horse, you will start to develop a clarity about the uniqueness of the horse before you, experience a deeper presence, a clearer awareness, a capacity to truly show up and feel into the horse's experience, a subtle attunement to the horse, and a capacity to tolerate and lean into difference, with openness and kindness.

Over time, this develops an understanding that all relationships require working with difficulty and ruptures, and you will start looking for relational conflict and challenge as an opportunity to know your horse in a deeper way. This is how your relationship will grow and become safer and more fulfilling over time, with presence, awareness, acceptance, curiosity and commitment. So here, we practice real Love.

Through these four capacities and attitudes, you will practice Love, in every moment of being together with the horse, every day. In this way, Love is operationalised in every experience. It is never just a thought nor is it something that is achieved or completed.

Love is a verb.

THE FIRST COMMITMENT: LOVE

THE SECOND COMMITMENT: VALUES

> It is important to be clear and to articulate your Values in relationship.

This happens organically in every meaningful relationship and in all long-term relationships.

It's essential to be clear about and ideally agree on your values (when there's the capacity to agree), with human-to-human relationships. But in interspecies relating, where there can't be verbal agreement, there becomes an even greater imperative to be very clear about the values that you have, that guide your responsibilities and your behaviour in all meaningful horse-human relationships. We as human animals have the frontal lobe and brain function to support cognition, meaning-making, to reflect and be intentional. Let's put this capacity to good use, in the service of our loved-ones, including our horses.

EXERCISE:
JOURNAL YOUR TOP 3 VALUES IN YOUR RELATIONSHIPS

Take 15 minutes to sit in a quiet space with a pen and paper and circle words listed on the following pages that represent the qualities, capacities or behaviours you most highly value, that guide your healthy, loving relationships.

This exercise is designed to support you to discover what it is that orients you in relationship, in all relationships that matter most to you.

The following list of words is not exhaustive, add as many of your own as you need.

Acceptance
Accomplishment
Accountability
Accuracy
Achievement
Adaptability
Adventurousness
Agreeableness
Alertness
Altruism
Ambition
Amiability
Amusement
Appreciative
Art
Articulateness
Assertiveness
Athleticism
Attentiveness
Authenticity
Awe
Balance
Beauty
Being admirable
Being dynamic
Being earnest
Being famous
Being folksy
Being frank
Being methodical
Being personable

Being reasonable
Being skilled
Being thoughtful
Being understanding
Benevolence
Big thinking
Bliss
Boldness
Bravery
Brilliance
Calmness
Candour
Capability
Carefulness
Caring
Cautiousness
Certainty
Challenge
Charisma
Charity
Charm
Cheerfulness
Citizenship
Clarity
Cleanliness
Clear-headedness
Cleverness
Comfort
Commitment
Common sense
Communication

Community
Compassion
Competence
Complexity
Confidence
Connection
Conscientiousness
Conservativeness
Consideration
Consistency
Constructiveness
Contemplation
Contentment
Contribution
Control
Conviction
Cooperation
Courage
Courteousness
Craftiness
Creativity
Credibility
Curiosity
Daringness
Decency
Decisiveness
Dedication
Deep thought
Democracy
Dependability
Determination

Devotion
Dignity
Diligence
Discipline
Discovery
Diversity
Drive
Dualism
Dutifulness
Easygoingness
Education
Effectiveness
Efficiency
Elegance
Eloquence
Emotional awareness
Emotional control
Empathy
Empowerment
Endurance
Energy
Enjoyment
Enthusiasm
Equality
Ethics
Excellence
Excitement
Expedience
Experimenting
Exploration
Expressiveness

THE SECOND COMMITMENT: VALUES

Extraordinary experiences	Gratitude	Justice	Patience
Fairness	Greatness	Kindness	Patriotism
Faith	Growth	Knowledge	Peace
Faithfulness	Happiness	Lawfulness	Peacefulness
Family	Hard work	Leadership	Performance
Farsightedness	Harmony	Learning	Perseverance
Fashion	Health	Liberty	Persistence
Feelings	Helpfulness	Life direction	Playfulness
Fidelity	Heroicness	Life experience	Pleasure
Flair	Honesty	Likability	Poise
Flexibility	Honour	Logic	Positive attitude
Focus	Hope	Love	Positivity
Foresight	Humbleness	Loyalty	Potential
Forgiving	Humility	Mastery	Power
Forthrightness	Humour	Maturity	Practicality
Fortitude	Idealism	Mellowness	Preciseness
Freedom	Imagination	Moderation	Principles
Freethinking	Incisiveness	Modesty	Productivity
Friendliness	Independence	Motivation	Professionalism
Friendship	Individualism	Neatness	Prosperity
Fun	Individuality	Neutrality	Protection
Fun-loving attitude	Influence	Newness	Punctuality
Generosity	Innovation	Niceness	Purpose
Gentleness	Insightfulness	Objectivity	Quality
Genuineness	Inspiration	Open-mindedness	Rationality
Giving	Integrity	Openness	Realism
Glamorousness	Intelligence	Optimism	Recognition
Good nature	Intensity	Order	Recreation
Goodness	Intuitiveness	Organisation	Reflection
Grace	Inventiveness	Originality	Relaxation
Graciousness	Joy	Passion	Reliability

Resourcefulness	Self-respect	Stability	Tolerance
Respect	Self-sufficiency	Status	Tradition
Respect for others	Selflessness	Steadiness	Tranquillity
Responsibility	Sensitivity	Strength	Transformation
Restraint	Serenity	Structure	Trust
Results-oriented	Service	Studiousness	Truth
Rigor	Simplicity	Success	Unity
Risk	Smarts	Sweetness	Variety
Romance	Sociability	Sympathy	Vivaciousness
Satisfaction	Social connection	Teamwork	Warmth
Security	Sophistication	Tenderness	Wealth
Self-awareness	Speed	Thoroughness	Well-roundedness
Self-improvement	Spirituality	Tidiness	Wisdom
Self-reliance	Spontaneity	Timeliness	Wit

In my personal therapy and self-discovery over the years, it has become clear that one of the things I most value in relationship is *passionate* love, a *love that is expressed actively* with affection and initiation towards the other. So, it may be construed as expressive love or active love or passionate love. I value this quality most highly in relationship.

The other thing I value highly is kindness. That includes the capacity to be kind - at times when I'm not feeling kind, when I might have feelings of frustration, anger, sadness, or fear (which I will absolutely want to be honest about and clear about and express in healthy ways with myself and others, as I can). But, above all, I wish to include kindness in all my relationships so that my feelings and the expression of my feelings do not harm the other.

Another value that's important to me is fairness. It's important that I honour the integrity of another's individuality, or uniqueness, or unique being, and that I do not prioritise my own pleasure or wellbeing or entitlement above another. This value of fairness supports me in remembering that we are all important, and we're all equally ordinary, equally wonderful and equally valuable.

Another value that I hold in high regard is freedom, and freedom of expression. It's been a lifelong journey for me personally, and to support my clients, my students, my family and my animal friends and family, to be able to safely and freely express their individuality and their uniqueness, in all of their potential. I hold freedom of expression and potentialising in very high regard. I don't feel I have the right to inhibit somebody's freedom of expression as long as it's safe, non-harming and a natural expression of their species and their individuality. This supports me to include an intention to foster the potentialising of the other, alongside the full expression of the other. It requires an honouring of space for the other, and providing and fostering an environment in which their potentialising can be well supported.

I hope this gives you a couple of examples of where you might start your personal reflections about your Values in relationship. Your values will be different to mine. Each of us have different temperaments, patterned ways of surviving and relating, as well as different histories, unique cultural, racial and gendered experiences which will inform the values that we each have or hold dear.

It's important to be really clear about your values, so that you have clear intentionality in your relationship with your horses and that when you transgress your values, have ruptures in relationship or behave in ways that violate your own values, you can hold yourself accountable in relationship to stay attentive, to stay true to and compliant with your own values, moral compass and ethics. This can support you to apologise, where needed, and find creative ways to meaningfully repair ruptures with the Others in your life who matter the most to you. This way you foster relationships that are intentional, committed and fulfilling. You will be leading a meaningful life full of nourishing relationships.

Personal Development

THE THIRD COMMITMENT: PERSONAL DEVELOPMENT

As a Horse Person and Horse Trainer - You are your best Tool.

(Of course you are not a tool, rather a being, but you get the picture!)

If your Tool is unaware, blunt, deadened, pessimistic, traumatised, insecurely attached, reflective, rigid, unsettled, frightened... this is the Tool You Use and Bring to Your Horses, and Horse Training!

If you were any other agent of change - like a psychotherapist, supporting growth and trauma healing, like a teacher, supporting children to learn about subjects in school and themselves – you would expect to be an educated, aware and skilful change maker (to meet the scope of practice as a psychotherapist or teacher, for example).

As a change maker for horses (to learn, grow and thrive in domesticated environments), you owe it to your horse, and the scope of practice of your horse work, to be an educated, aware and skilful Tool! (Again, human being, of course, but you get the metaphor!)

So, let's focus on what a **Personally-Developed Horse Person looks like**.

SELF-AWARENESS

Self-awareness is essential for any good horse person.

Self-awareness includes awareness of self-experience in the present moment, and awareness of patterned ways of thinking, believing and behaving.

So, awareness of self-experience means I am aware of:

- ❏ my nervous system and the present moment (feeling settled, calm and regulated or unsettled, triggered or overwhelmed and dysregulated).
- ❏ my feelings (fear, anger, sadness, joy, vulnerability, frustration) in the present moment.
- ❏ my thoughts in the present moment (including the self-talk and thoughts that I'm offering myself in any moment about myself, other context, the world).

- ❏ my body, including my body sensations, throughout my entire body from the top of my head to the tips of each toe, my *felt sense*.
- ❏ my breath, where I breathe into my body, how I breathe, how I interrupt my breathing, my tendencies in breathing.
- ❏ my behaviour, my posture, my movement, my use of body in the service of acting, actions, interacting and patterned ways of relating with others and the environment.

THE THIRD COMMITMENT: PERSONAL DEVELOPMENT

EXERCISE:
START A SELF-AWARENESS JOURNAL WITH THE FOLLOWING 6 CATEGORIES:

1. Nervous state
2. Breath and Breathing
3. Body Sensations
4. Feelings
5. Thoughts
6. Posture, Movement, Action.

Record with date, time, the data (that you notice)

Example entry:

26/2/23 9.20am

Breath & Breathing - I noticed my breathing was shallow and tended to be up around my chest and shoulders this morning, as I met my horse.

Feelings - I notice excitement (joy) and fear. I noticed Fear through my heart rate increase and sensations in my chest. The Fear felt not too intense, probably like a 4/10. Excitement felt bubbly and about a 7/10.

Thoughts - I kept thinking about my Horse, whether he liked me, whether I was doing the right thing, whether I was doing the right thing with the horse training exercise I was doing (leading exercise). My thoughts were dominating my approach and looping around constantly. I did notice a time when my thoughts went quiet – I was noticing the smell of my horse. Hmm!

Behaviour - I noticed I tried walking up to meet my horse with my square shoulders (I have been noticing I slump a bit, and I carry a lot of tension in my shoulders, a lot of the time), and I was thinking 'breathe, be soft, be open, notice!' I used an outbreath to let down, and laughed out loud. My horse looked at me and starting walking to me.

Body Sensations - I noticed when the above happened, I became aware of the tension in my shoulders and jaw eased off a bit, especially when I smiled, laughed and sighed. I want to track my sensations in my body more!

Pattern Awareness

Self-awareness requires not just a capacity to track the above data in the present moment (nervous state, feelings, thoughts, body sensations, behaviour and movement) but also awareness of (and ideally an understanding of) our *own patterns, ongoing tendencies, habits or patterned ways of experiencing, being, relating and behaving over time.*

Cognitive patterns include thinking patterns. These are the tendencies that we have about *the thoughts that we offer ourselves*, what the content of those thoughts are, whether they're in touch with reality to some degree or out of touch of reality, whether they're kind, whether they're critical, judgemental or cruel in nature, whether they're looping, repetitive, whether they're present-related or past-related, and how they tend to arrive, in the context of current environments, others or field-based conditions.

Cognitive patterns also include beliefs. These are tricky to track, unless you get some support around tracking your beliefs—what you believe about yourself (self-beliefs), what you believe about others (other-beliefs), and what you believe about the world (world-beliefs).

Personal development, psychotherapy, life coaching and self-help practices increase your tendency to be aware of your patterns, your cognitive patterns, the ways that you tend to think, and the patterns you have in thoughts and beliefs. *Your thoughts, thinking and beliefs fundamentally shape your orienting, perception, behaviour and relating.* These cognitive patterns will be unaware or unconscious, until the moment you become aware of them (through focus, intention and hard work).

So, the self-aware person has access to their present moment's experience, across their nervous system, their body, their feeling, their movement, and their sensing. The self-aware person is also aware of their tendencies and the patterned ways they tend to think, cognise and believe. The self-aware person also has a clear understanding of how they tend to behave in relationship. For example, whether they agree with others, or disagree with others. If they have a dull and desensitised connection to self-body, and others and their bodies, if they are overly intellectualised, or preoccupied with life as a joke, or life as a running sequence of thoughts, narratives, stories etc.

Now, the self-aware person, the person who has done this personal development work has access to both their *experience in the present moment*, and their *patterned ways of thinking, believing and behaving in relationship*, as they arrive in the present moment. The self-aware person is aware in the present moment, and engages in reflection, after the experience.

So, all this personal self-awareness and personal development sits as container and *context for all your horse relationships*. Whatever you do (in yourself, in relationship to other people in life) you will bring a variation of these patterns (or different patterns) into your interactions and relationship with horses.

THE THIRD COMMITMENT: PERSONAL DEVELOPMENT

EXERCISE:
TAKE A MOMENT TO REFLECT ON THE FOLLOWING QUESTIONS AND INQUIRY

Do you approach the world from a fundamental position of:

The world is safe. (World-belief)

I am safe. (Self-belief)

The world is unsafe. (World-belief)

The world is dangerous. (World-belief)

I can trust others. (Other-belief)

I cannot trust others. (Other-belief)

People are unsafe and animals are safe. (Other-belief)

Men are dangerous. (Other-belief)

People are out to get me. (Other-belief)

People are fundamentally good. (Other-belief)

I am okay. (Self-belief)

I am flawed. (Self-belief)

I am bad. (Self-belief)

I am wrong. (Self-belief)

I am stupid. (Self-belief)

I am better than others. (Self-belief)

I am superior. (Self-belief)

People are stupid. (Other-belief)

Animals are more intelligent than people. (Other-belief)

Animals are safe. (Other-belief)

Horses are stupid. (Other-belief)

Horses are intelligent. (Other-belief)

Horses are spiritual beings. (Other-belief)

Horses are healers. (Other-belief)

Horses have no feelings. (Other-belief)

EXERCISE:

I invite you to just pause and reflect on any of the above beliefs as examples, and how they would, if left unaware, fundamentally shape a person's perception, approach, behaviour, relating, thinking, feeling, nervous state, and overall ability to function in the world, as well as their likelihood to harm others or harm one's-self. I am hoping you are now, upon reflection, starting to understand why *being aware of your patterns or patterned ways of cognising and behaving, will fundamentally shape everything you do and how you interact with your horse.* How you approach your horse, interact, how you train, and how your horses experience you is shaped by your patterns. What are your Beliefs? Start a reflection Journal.

THE THIRD COMMITMENT: PERSONAL DEVELOPMENT

The self-aware person, or the person on a personal development journey, seeks to be openly curious and to be monitoring and tracking their experience, their patterned ways of relating (thinking and behaving) and their impact on others. They understand that they are continually shaping or co-creating their relationships with others, human and horse (and all non-human mammals) via their patterned ways of relating and aware relating.

EXERCISE:
TAKE A MOMENT TO REFLECT ON THE FOLLOWING QUESTIONS AND INQUIRY

How do I tend to relate to others and the world?

Do I tend to relate to the world in a sensitive hypersensitive way, hyper-vigilant way or a desensitised way?

Do I tend to relate to others from a fixed position of being preoccupied by my own thoughts of, "I am less than, or I'm not good enough," or, "I'm better than," or, "I'm superior to?"

Do I have a preoccupation with my 'thinking about' or analysing anything, everything, all the time and therefore find it rare to just 'be' in the moments of relating, rather than 'thinking through' all moments of relating?

Do I tend to relate to the world and others from a place of held in energy, where I am holding back feelings, words, tendencies? Or Do I tend to relate from a place of expression, spontaneity and fluidity?

Do I relate to others in the world with a degree of impulsivity or violence? Or Do I relate with others in the world (children, adults, animals, horses) in a way that assumes I am responsible for everything I encounter, and everything is my fault, or my responsibility?

Journal your Behavioural or Relational patterns.

> # EXERCISE:
> ## TAKE A MOMENT TO REFLECT ON THE FOLLOWING QUESTIONS AND INQUIRY
>
> How do I *impact the people I'm in relationship with?*
>
> How do I *impact the horses I'm in relationship with?*
>
> Have you noticed that your horse might respond to you in a different way than to your neighbour, to your friends, your coach, mentor?
>
> What are my *tendencies and patterned ways of relating* with my horses?
>
> Are they serving the horse well? Serving our relationship well?
>
> *In general, reflect on how you might you seek support as you dive further into this self-discovery work.*

I have met many horse people in the journey of educating people about equine assisted psychotherapy (EAP) and equine assisted learning (EAL). Given that EAP and EAL practitioners will be relating to various clients, including children, vulnerable adults, clients with trauma, neurodiverse clients and those with a range of psychological, psychiatric and relationship challenges, it is imperative they do significant personal development work to ensure they are able to relate in an I-Thou manner, bring empathy, affect attunement and to support others in times of stress, trauma, complexity and skill-development.

Over the last decade of training students, I have noticed certain patterns amongst my students. Whilst I work and believe in an approach that sees all patterns as unique and intelligent solutions with systemic or structural (intersectional) origins, in the service of being succinct and clear, in this book, I will share some generalisations and trends I have noticed, drawn from my own experiences as a trainer and educator. What I notice is that the students who have commonly done very little or no personal reflection or personal development work, tend to self-identify or behave in more of a rigid, righteous or purist manner. They can have a tendency to shame, blame and complain or be aggressive toward self or others. People who have done significant personal development work tend to be more open, curious, and are able to be vulnerable, spontaneous, playful, discerning (rather than rigid), and may be more aware of their limitations, strengths and self-experience. I have noticed these individuals also know how to contain themselves and express themselves, intentionally and choicefully.

THE THIRD COMMITMENT: PERSONAL DEVELOPMENT

The student who has *not undertaken personal development work* can present in a multitude of diverse ways including being overly attached to being right, in control, being inflexible or rigid and having a tendency to not to show their feelings. These students may or may not have trauma histories, or complex histories that are well managed and quite functional, and can present as rigid, or in one fixed way, regardless of the situation or external factors. In the context of EAP and EAL training, some of the *non-personally developed* horse-people can present with *inflexibility* their behaviour and are more rigid or polarised on one side of the behavioural continuum.

For example:

The Narcissistic Horse Person – Superior to others and always know what's right. Teaches through 'story-telling', jokes and humour that puts others down and elevates self.

The Self-Critical Horse Person – Over-responsibility pattern that perceives all horse's feelings and behaviours as a result of themselves (and their flaws). Dominant self-talk is, "It's my fault."

The Spiritual Horse Person – Sees the horse as saviour, healer and all-knowing other. Cannot meet basic species-specific needs of horse, as interpretations obscure reality.

The Scientific Horse Person – The horse is reduced to a set of behaviours to be reinforced or shaped. Conceptual and task-focused and has an emphasis on right and wrong or being correct.

The Feelings Horse Person – Passive and waits for horse. Worried about horse's feelings.

The Seeking a Guru Horse Person – Needs to be told what to do, by an 'expert' or 'whisperer'.

The Intellectualised Horse Person – Relates to horses from a cognitive and reflective, meaning-making place of insight and little embodiment or emotional skill.

The Traumatised Horse Person – one of the following four may present:

> *Desensitised* – Unaware of horses' nervous system and feelings.
>
> *Chaotic* – Unable to learn, as lives in chaos and learning can't be integrated or practiced.
>
> *Frightened* – Obsessed with horse safety, unconscious displacement of own fear and need to be in control, judging others as safe or unsafe.
>
> *Frightening / Violent* – Behaviour with horses evidences a tendency for heavy-handedness, low frustration tolerance, force and violence. This person may kick, pull, whip, strike, aggress and harm the horse.

Remember, the above patterns are a part of human nature and in and of themselves are not wrong or bad, only rigid. They are fixed, patterned ways of thinking and relating to life, and horses. It is a part of human nature to, sometimes, be self-critical, narcissistic, intellectualised, feeling-centred, scientifically focused, spiritually-focused and so forth. If these patterns stay polarised, fixed and unaware, this is when things become problematic for the person, and the horse. In a fixed position or pattern (as listed above), the relating is limited, not creatively adapting to the present moment, and by extension (to varying degrees depending on the pattern) can be harmful for the horse.

I am listing these patterns here to help you self-identify, to support your open curiosity and to kick-start or expand your personal work, if you so choose. If you choose to be in relationship with horses or train horses, I believe it is your responsibility to personally develop, grow and be the most supported, aware, reflective, adaptive and healthy version of yourself, that you can be. For your horses, and for yourself.

It is a life-long journey, and as I always say to my students, "You have the rest of your life to do this." So, give yourself the next three decades at least, to do your personal work! Get some good support. As a herd animal, we were never meant to do this alone! ●

THE THIRD COMMITMENT: PERSONAL DEVELOPMENT

EXERCISE:
SELF AWARENESS SNAPSHOT JOURNAL

Journal each day with a snapshot of your current Awareness capacity.
Be honest with yourself, as honest as you can tolerate!

Examples:

"As of today, I'm in touch with my fear in the present moment. I can feel my nervous system - the activating through pulsating around my chest, my heart rate has gone up."

"Today I can sense my feet on the ground. I can tune into the environment through my five senses."

"I'm aware of my tendency in relationship with my partner with critical thinking or responding in a controlling manner."

"Today I noticed a tendency to respond in a people pleasing manner I said yes when I meant no."

Journal your reflections at the end of each day a snapshot of your current Un-awareness areas.

"I am un-aware of…"

"My head is aching and I am guessing I did not notice when my head started aching today."

"I feel confused…I am not sure if I am frightened, angry, frustrated or sad."

"I helped out a friend today and feel exhausted, I wonder if I have a pattern of over-responsibility or people-pleasing?"

"My horse had her ears back at me today, I wonder if I was unaware of my nervous system and I was stressed or whether there were feelings I was ignoring like fear?"

Every time you go out to be with your horse, take an internal note, and when you come inside add an entry in your journal with the date that tracks your self-awareness and curiosity.

The horse person on a personal development journey is intentional, focused and clear.

HORSES, LOVE & SCIENCE

So, in summary, with support, time, self-care and dedication, you can be more of a *conscious, aware horseperson*.

You bring all this self-awareness into your conscious and intentional horse-human relationships, for the benefit of You, your Horse, and your *relationship with your horses*.

This personal development work will magnify your part of the relational equation, and it will support your relating overall. It will benefit your horses so much.

The more aware you are, *the safer you are* for your horses.

The more aware you are, the clearer your requests will become. The clearer the communications, the clearer the requests, the kinder the requests will be, the better timed they will be, the more attuned you will be, and the more *in touch with reality you will be!* You can't go wrong with that, can you?

Do it for Yourself and do it for your horses.

This personal work is an important *personal investment*, as it will support your capacity for an intimate, reality-based relationship with your horse, and all other people!

EXERCISE:

SEEK THE SUPPORT YOU NEED, BECAUSE YOU ARE A HERD ANIMAL TOO AND DESERVE TO FEEL, AND BE UNDERSTOOD AND SUPPORTED.

You deserve all the support you need - find a good counsellor, psychotherapist, equine assisted psychotherapist or equine assisted learning practitioner, a life coach, or a support person that helps you to become aware of your self-experience—in your body and your nervous system, your feelings, your posture and your movement, your behaviour, your wants, needs and values, and your patterned ways of thinking, your deeper beliefs (self-beliefs, other-beliefs, world-beliefs) and your patterned behaviours in relationship.

You deserve and need support. We all do.

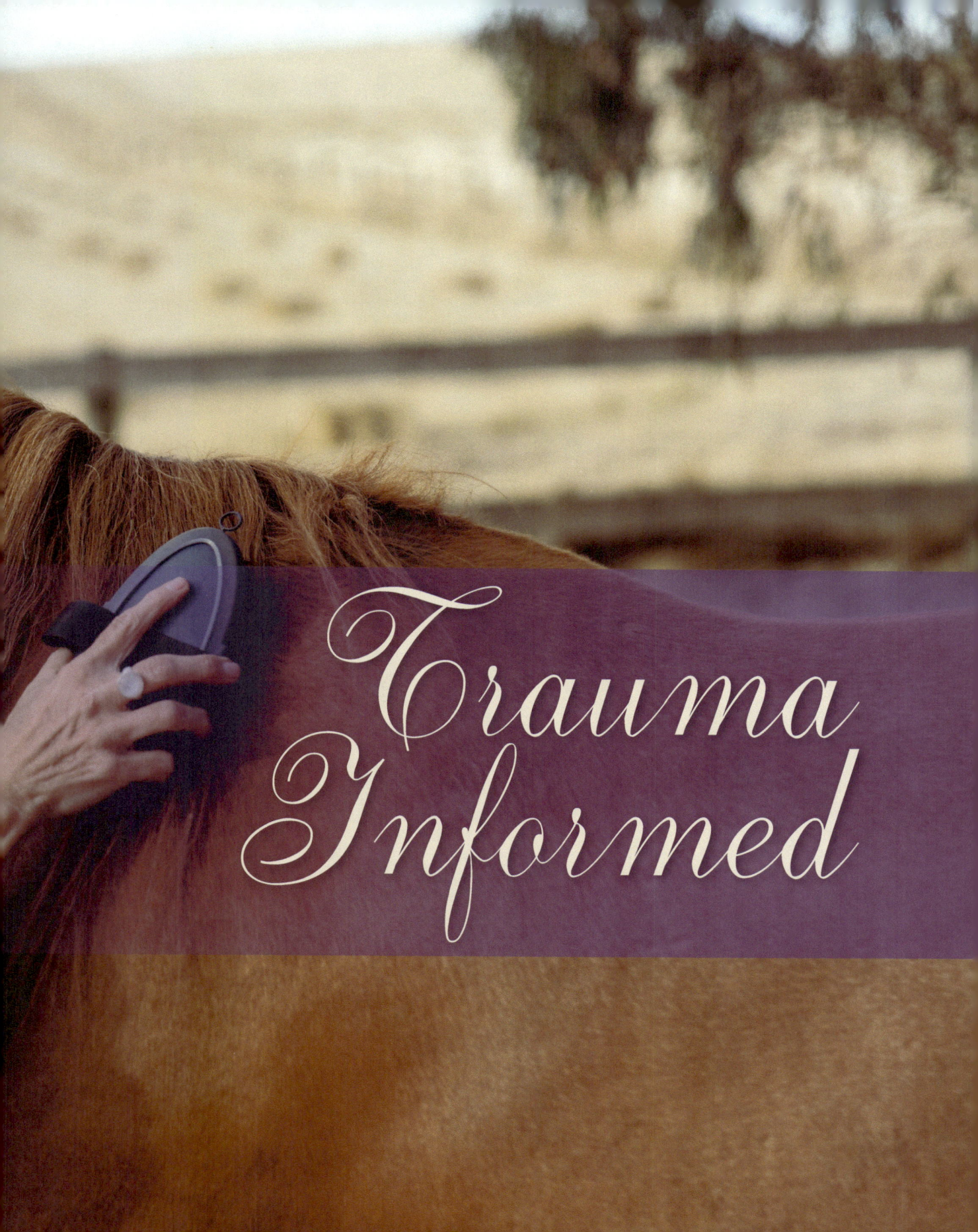
Trauma Informed

HORSES, LOVE & SCIENCE

THE FOURTH COMMITMENT: TRAUMA-INFORMED

> ## TRACK YOUR HORSE'S EXPERIENCE AND EXPRESSION OF TRAUMA, STRESS SIGNALS AND RELAXATION SIGNALS AND IMPROVE YOUR INTER-SPECIES RELATING AND TRAINING

Horses experience fight, flight, freeze and other survival states or energies, in the same way humans do and like us, can also engage in management or defensive strategies to cope with these experiences (Schlote, 2017). The terms fight, flight and freeze are becoming more commonly known and used and it is helpful to understand what these states or energies actually refer to, both in our horses and ourselves. These nervous system states can be understood using Stephen Porges' Polyvagal Theory, introduced in 1994. Polyvagal Theory offers a model of the social mammal's nervous system that includes the Sympathetic Nervous System (SNS) and Parasympathetic Nervous System (PNS) (Porges, 1995). The SNS is responsible for activating energy (arousal) and action, including a social mammal's fight or flight response whilst the PNS is responsible for both regulation (also known as Ventral Vagal or the 'rest and digest' state), as well as the 'shutdown' or freeze response (known as Dorsal Vagal state). When a social mammal, like a horse or a human, does not have adequate support, time, space, and safety, or is exposed to ongoing stress, the ability to naturally express themselves freely and discharge the excess survival energy from the body (through natural fight or flight responses, for example), they can become chronically dysregulated or 'stuck' in the Sympathetic Nervous System (hyperarousal) states or Dorsal Vagal (hypoarousal) states. In humans, this may be expressed and labelled as Generalised Anxiety (SNS), Depression (Dorsal Vagal) or Post Traumatic Stress Disorder. Similar, albeit species-specific, symptoms and behaviours can be present in horses too. Horses can present in in chronic stressed states (with ulcers and ill-health), in chronic or persistent fear states (easily frightened, shying, hyper-vigilant), in rigid freeze responses and states, with dissociative tendencies, and in collapsed freeze states presenting as lethargic, depressed, shut down and learned helplessness. Horses that are in collapsed freeze states and learned helplessness will appear quiet and well-behaved to the ignorant horse-person, however, when viewed through a trauma-informed lens, are more accurately understood to be traumatised as a result of being exposed to inescapable, chronic stress and aversive experiences (which may include neglect, mis-handling, abuse or violence).

Where do we start if we own, support, train or live with a horse with trauma or ourselves experience trauma? The eight commitments of I-Thou horsepersonship are an excellent place to start and provide a good foundation for you and your horses' safety and wellbeing. You may also wish to seek out specialist support and training in trauma, and luckily there are some excellent learning opportunities available for horse-owners. The Equine Psychotherapy Institute provides an excellent specialist training in understanding trauma in ourselves and our human clients in equine assisted psychotherapy, and Equusoma provides comprehensive training in horse-human trauma recovery.

For the everyday horse-person, learning to track your horse's nervous system is a must. Start by learning to know when your horse is stressed, when your horse is relaxed, when your horse is activated, when your horse is overwhelmed or dysregulated, and how to support your horse to re-regulate their nervous system (become settled again) is a must for all horse people, and is an essential, fundamental skill of the I-Thou Horse Person. This requires specific awareness of the stress signals of your horse, the relaxation signals of your horse and a support toolkit you can use whenever you and your horse need it. Start to develop a toolkit to support your horse to re-regulate their nervous system once they are close to the edge of their tolerance or you have unintentionally stressed or triggered the horse to feel activated, stressed, overwhelmed or dysregulated. Not all stress is bad, in fact stress is a normal part of learning and life. Arousal moves along a continuum from relaxed to alert and focused to stressed, however, it is not really a linear continuum, but more like an orchestra of changing arousal states and systems. To engage and learn we need a degree of arousal and attentiveness. But to relate with and educate a horse, we must be able to read their attentive or alert state, that maintains a degree of relaxation. We must be able to read the fear signals, the stress signals, the state of attentiveness or arousal that is relaxed, and know when our horses are likely in pain, in stress or in a traumatised state. First, what we need to learn about is each individual horse's window of tolerance.

Window of Tolerance

The window of tolerance describes the best state of 'arousal' or stimulation in which we (and other non-human mammals, such as horses) are able to function and thrive in everyday life. When we exist within this window, we are able to learn effectively, play, and relate well to ourselves and others (Siegel, 2010).

Trauma and cumulative stress can 'shrink' our window of tolerance, which means it doesn't take much for our nervous system to feel overwhelmed (dysregulated) and move into fight, flight, immobility or freeze (hyperarousal or hypoarousal).

People can develop resources to support and re-regulate in the immediate moments of hyperarousal (e.g., fear and panic) or hypoarousal (e.g., disassociation, lethargy, freeze or collapse). Over time, as people develop these supports, they can start to broaden their window of tolerance and increase their capacity to experience emotions and stressful situations and events, without becoming dysregulated (i.e., stuck in panic reaction or dissociative reaction).

THE FOURTH COMMITMENT: TRAUMA-INFORMED

Your Horse's Window of Tolerance

What is tolerable for one horse may be intolerable for another horse. This is the window, or comfort zone that is *within the individual horse's capacity to concentrate, focus, relate and learn*. It is unique to every individual horse, depending on their temperament, their history, their trauma history, and their current skills, capacities and level of training.

Essentially, the window of tolerance provides a map for what is tolerable for your horse, what is within their comfort zone, what is on the edge of their comfort zone, or outside their comfort zone (uncomfortable, intolerable or overwhelming).

The only way you can track your horse's window of tolerance is via observing nonverbal cues and behavioural communications.

The horse can't tell you what is OK and what is not OK in words - you need to track their *breathing*, their *eyes*, their *posture*, the change in *behaviour*, their *shift in the movement* of their body, their *biomechanics*, and overall use of their body.

Recognising Fear, Stress, Relaxation and Pain is vital. I have included some examples below. Additionally, you can research more about recognising pain in horses in daily life and in ridden horses. If you ride, it is your responsibility to know the pain indicators, and the relaxation markers, for your horse's welfare, wellbeing and enrichment.

Fear Signals

Horses can display signs of fear by:

- Lifting head
- Looking toward novel or scary object
- Showing white (sclera) of eye
- Flaring or widening nostril
- Lifting tail
- Snorting
- Walking with tension in the body
- Engaging in flight responses such as running away, spinning, shying etc.

STRESS SIGNALS

Examples could include (depending on context):
- Shallow breathing
- Tight jaw, tight facial muscles, tight, tense, stiff movements
- High pulse
- Yawning, Lick and Chew (release post stressful event/arousal event)
- Manure may be soft, runny or there may be copious amounts
- Sclera of eye showing, 'worried' eyes
- Trembling, shaking
- Bucking, Bolting, Rearing
- Shying (Can signal fear, stress, pain or trauma)
- Appeasement behaviours, such as looking away
- Displacement behaviours, such as pawing when tied up

Long term Stress and Trauma examples:
- Stall, yard or paddock walking or pacing up and down and other stereotypic behaviours, such as windsucking
- Teeth grinding
- Weight Loss
- Tail swishing, clamping
- Biting at girth, at handler
- Colic
- Sweating
- Chewing or biting, biting wood
- Freezing behaviours and hypoarousal responses like shut down, listlessness, depression and learned helplessness

THE PAIN FACE INDICATORS (GLEERUP ET AL., 2015)

- Orbital tightening around eye
- Wrinkles above eye
- Sclera visible
- Half blinking
- Mouth opening
- Muzzle pulled and pressed up
- Nostrils open wide and square
- Wrinkle between nostrils
- Lower lip retracted
- Ears wide at base, lowered outwards
- Worried eye or tense stare

RELAXATION SIGNALS (EXAMPLES COULD INCLUDE, DEPENDING ON CONTEXT)

- Soft or supple musculature or posture
- Head and neck in mid to mid-low position
- Hindleg may be cocked if standing
- Slow meandering walking if grazing
- Occasional snorts (let down breaths)
- Suppleness in facial muscles
- Long nostrils
- Almond-shaped eyes, with no creases above eye lids
- Loose lips
- Ears moving front to back (not pricked, pinned or floppy at sides)
- Soft and flat chin
- Tail hanging loosely
- Attentive to environment
- Curious, Seeking interaction
- Allogrooming in herd
- Soft muscles in movement

It is an essential capacity and skill to be tracking *your horses fear, stress, pain and present moment window of tolerance.*

You can only do this through observation over time, with patience, and being openly curious and open to seeing, sensing and noticing, NOT by assuming, thinking and labelling too soon.

Every single horse in my herd of 13 has a very different display of fear, stress and pain. Similarly, their unique window of tolerance for cues, pressure, exposure, relating, novelty, and for learning something new differs too.

It's important that you understand your horse's window of tolerance, and the uniqueness of their window of tolerance and that you stay well within their window of what is OK for them.

Learning happens inside the window of tolerance, which may include interest, activation, curiosity, seeking, play or relaxation. When horses (or humans!) move outside of their window of tolerance, they have become overwhelmed and they're no longer able to concentrate, sense, function optimally and learn.

Every time you are with your horse is an opportunity to intentionally track the horses window of tolerance, notice their activation levels, and track what level of activation or arousal is OK and manageable for them? What is at their edge? What is not OK? Relating and learning must include relaxation and low arousal levels that rise, and fall.

Horse Support Toolkit

Start to build your **trauma-informed 'Horse Support' toolkit**. This involves building many *ways to promote relaxation and a settled nervous system* as a fundamental approach and skill. Secondly, it requires *developing techniques to use when they are needed in the moment.* So, this requires asking yourself how you re-regulate your horse's nervous system once they have become activated, stressed and close to overwhelmed (frightened, confused or unclear, too heightened in energy), where they are unable to focus and concentrate or learn.

Tracking the fear stress signals that are present and tracking their escalation is an important skill.

So, your horse is in an activation cycle – What do you see? What are the *early warning signs, and the fear and stress signals? What are the signs they are escalating*, not deescalating?

How do you *support them into an activation-deactivation part of the cycle*? How do you trigger or support a *relaxation response*, right now?

Some of the common techniques that you can use may include some of the following:

THE FOURTH COMMITMENT: TRAUMA-INFORMED

EXERCISE:
BUILDING YOUR HORSE'S RELAXATION, STRESS & WOT SUPPORT TOOLKIT

Choose one of your horses and document his or her:

- **Relaxation signals**
- **Fear & Stress signals**
- **WOT** - Window of Tolerance signifiers, including behaviours exhibited when in flight response, hyperreactive, overwhelmed and dysregulated, or unavailable for learning and relating
- **Support Toolkit** – list your active supports to soothe, settle, regulate your horse.

Reflect on :

- How does my horse look when they are relaxed, comfortable, content?
- What is happening in their eyes, face, body, behaviour, approach, tendencies?
- How would you describe the softness in the eye, in the body and the muscles, in the gait and movement, or in the stillness in the positioning of the body?
- How would you describe the body language and the communication of fear responses and stress signals?
- How does your horse appear at the edge of their 'window of tolerance'? e.g., in the eye, in the behaviour, in the sounds and movement and tendencies of your horse?
- What do they look like? How are they behaving? How are they moving? What is their head carriage and the shape of their back and the movement and the length of their stride and the gait?
- Describe it as fully and descriptively as you possibly can manage.
- What do you see when your horse in an overwhelmed dysregulated state? Be specific.

Support Toolkit

- Pause, wait, or stop what you are doing.
- Offer yourself a letdown breath, ground yourself
- Offer Horse the 'let down' breath, to co-regulate
- Wait for your horse to breathe out, or lick and chew, shake, snort, soften in the eye.
- It might be giving Distance and Space, by stepping back and away.
- It may be Stepping Closer, or cuing Slow down or Stop
- It might be Stroking, Touching or Wither Massaging
- It might be soft, Soothing Talk, "It's OK" with calm, regulated tone of voice
- It might be lowering the horse's head
- It might be giving Distance, Space and Time- So, it might not include proximity or touch, but the opposite, for your horse!

I am not in favour of putting fingers in the horses' mouth or systematically neck yielding, as a ritualised response to regulate the horse. I find these techniques and others, can be experienced as intrusive or not a good fit for the individual horse or or the specific situation, further triggering an unintentional escalation of the nervous system (a fear or stress arousal).

Relaxation and low Arousal levels are the Key

Focus on what supports your horse to be settled, relaxed, interested, seeking and content. It is your job to support, relax, settle and re-regulate the horse, once they have become frightened, stressed, overwhelmed, or activated to the degree that they're no longer able to concentrate, learn or be safely with you. Fear responses once learned can become permanent due to potentiation and the horse's excellent memory. It is such an important principle to avoid fear, and avoid inadvertently practicing flight responses like startling, running or bolting away. Make it a priority to look for *relaxation responses, soft eyes, soft body, soft muscles, loose, flowing movement. This is the calm place for you and your horse (when energy levels are low and higher!)*

The only way to do this is by being Present and Tracking. Tracking the horse's body language and communications, their comfort zones, tracking the edge of tolerance and the window of tolerance. Additionally, it is vital to track the horse's experience of being activated, dysregulated or overwhelmed. Tracking your horse's prey responses of fear, his or her affiliative behaviours of seeking, curiosity, play, relaxation and resting are important. Experiment with tracking these tendencies when your horse is with you, interacting with you, and when you are observing your horse from afar. This way you can observe your *horse's tendencies around you as well as in their natural environment (ie in their grazing paddock)*, in their herd and away from human interaction, human presence and human-related contexts.

Become crystal clear of what the horse's nervous system is communicating to you, and what they need, and then you can put your supports to good use in the moment the horse needs them.

Depending on their individuality and history, some horses need more affection, touch and close proximity. Some horses need more freedom to move, space and distance. Some horses will need particular environments and pair bonds, proximity to the herd, and specific spaces and places and contexts. Find what your horse needs.

Stress is experienced differently by different horses depending on genetics, temperament, motivational state, history of trauma, and experience with people, and horse training experiences. Stress will result from not having the basic species needs met in their housing and environment (ie isolation and separation, insufficient movement and access to fibre, hay) and from unethical handling or horse training / equitation that was confusing, included conflicting signals, strong or intolerable pressure, frightening situations, no escape to relentless aids (pulling on bit, mouth, kicking), pressure, pain (related to training techniques) or punishment and violence (smacking, whipping, yelling, hitting). In these circumstances the horse (with a new owner) will quickly revert to hyperactive states or freeze states, including shutdown, collapse or learned helplessness, appearing listless and depressed.

Arousal that includes interest or attention may include release of adrenaline, producing momentary increase in blood pressure, heart rate, activation and flight tendencies, however this can be managed successfully with the tracking of the nervous system, window of tolerance, use of support toolkit and re-instating the relaxation and settling part of the cycle of experience (within a couple of minutes).

Overactive arousal, stress experienced over a long period of time and leads to release of the chemical cortisol, which does not dissipate quickly, but may take hours to settle in the short term, and may need to be managed for the horses' life, depending on the traumatic history. Longer term stress and trauma will impact the gut and immune system (ulcers and colic, for example), and support the development of what's called antipredator behaviours (like bucking, bolting or shying).

McLean (2022) recommends to learn to recognise fearful behaviour, understand the potentiation of fear, maintain low arousal levels, avoid practicing fear and flight responses, like out of control lungeing, use slowing signals, ensure horse training includes light aids, consistent, precise, and well-timed releases of pressure (pressure-release learning), correct use of positive reinforcement (touch , food, freedom), understanding stereotypic behaviours, and indicators of pain, in a broader context of understanding Equitation Science's ten principles (of which we will overview in the science chapter).

Stress is a very big topic, however, your trauma-informed lens and I-Thou Horsepersonship will support your ethical relating and horse training. Rachel Draaisma's work on calming signals and pacifying behaviours of horses (Draaisma, 2017) is a good support.

Keep your horse's nervous state, affective and mental state squarely in your mind at all times. This way you can constantly assess your horse's arousal, fear, stress and relaxation states, and prioritise keeping your horse well inside their window of tolerance, whilst meeting their species-specific needs and engaging in intentional training or relating. Developing your Horse Support Toolkit means you have this ready to support your horse, when they need you most.

THE FOURTH COMMITMENT: TRAUMA-INFORMED

Phenomenology

THE FIFTH COMMITMENT: PHENOMENOLOGY

> THE I-THOU HORSEPERSON IS MOST INTERESTED IN THE PHENOMENA OF THE HORSES, THAT IS, THE HORSE'S EXPERIENCE OF BEING A HORSE!

Phenomenology is the study of subjective experience, and it is the focus on direct, immediate, subjective experience. It's interested in minimising any habitual ways we may distort or cloud our perception of the inner experience, other, or the outer world by use of automatic assumption, interpretation, opinion, theories, judgments, positions and biases.

Phenomenology attempts to discover the world in its felt immediacy and direct truth, through the study of the phenomenon, phenomena, self-phenomena and other-phenomena.

In phenomenology, we understand that each of us perceive, construct, and construe reality differently and uniquely, hence, there are no experts on another's experience. We are interested in the primary phenomena or data unfolding.

When we use phenomenology as an approach as a horseperson, we utilise four specific skills and capacities of the phenomenologically-oriented practitioner, and, we use phenomenological inquiry and phenomenological observation.

In phenomenological inquiry with a person-to-person psychotherapy context, we can inquire into the experience of the other and support the expression of the client's unique and subjective experience. Through the inquiry process, the Other has an opportunity to experience and know themselves, feel themselves, explore themselves, and unfolding self-experience, in an even deeper way (had the inquiry process not happened). Part of this inquiry process is verbal and part is non-verbal or experiential.

Clearly, we can't ask our horses verbal questions, but we can bring the spirit of the phenomenological method of inquiry into our approach with horses. We can be asking questions, through non-verbal conversations or dialogue, where we 'ask' a question by making a request (e.g., Would you like to come to me?) or communicating some way (e.g., Turning your attention from the environment in general, and orienting, looking and gazing gently at one of your horse-friends in the paddock), and then stay openly curious, observing and tracking the responses of the horse closely (utilising our four capacities of the phenomenological practitioner, which I will introduce). The horse's answers will be communicated through their non-verbal body language responses, communications and behaviour in the present moment (from subtle to more overt responses, shifts, changes and expressions).

We can utilise this phenomenological approach by - noticing, observing, tracking closely, being open and curious, and available to 'hear' via the skills and the attitude of the phenomenological practitioner.

The phenomenological horse person intends to cultivate an open, not knowing, non-striving, curiosity that supports an open, allowing, receptive vessel or vehicle to *track the experience, wants, motivators and behaviours of the horse*. The phenomenological horse person does this without trying to change, judge, or label what they are observing or moving to assumption, interpretation, analysing or theorising too soon! Linking the dots and using labelling too prematurely acts to block the horse person's capacity to observe more fully at first, without know 'why'.

This degree of open curiosity and honesty means that we are open to not knowing. The I-Thou horseperson approaches the horse in the present moment, *in every moment of interchange* and interaction with their horse or horses, with an orientation of genuine curiosity, such as

"Who are you in this present moment?"

"What are you sensing?"

"What are you experiencing?"

"What are you feeling?"

"What are you wanting?"

"What are you doing?"

"How does it feel if you move like this?"

"What happens to you, when I offer that...what do you experience here?"

Instead of a verbal reply, maybe the horse will respond with their whole being and body to the approach, to the relating, to the person's presence, communications or requests, to particular cues or stimuli, so we can track the phenomena of the horse.

Example Horse Phenomena we may track could include:

- A shift in the horse's orientation or movement
- Change in the expression of a body part
- Widening of the eye
- Closing of the eye
- Relaxing of the eye muscles
- Tensing of the eye muscles
- Minute changes in the nostrils
- A Lift of the wither
- Sinking of the chest

- Closing or Clamping of the tail
- A re-orientation toward a different direction
- A change in how the horse orients to the environment
- A change in how the horse orients to the other (animal, horse or human)
- Turning toward the person
- Turning away from the person
- Turning away from the herd
- Turning toward the herd
- And lots more!

So, we have this attitude of open, spacious curiosity as we are approaching the horse, as we are relating and communicating with the horse via our attention, orientation and behaviour, as we're making requests of the horse, and we're discovering the truth in the present moment. We are discovering this truth as we are observing, tracking and reading the horse's nonverbal body language, responses and communications.

This is incredibly precious and highly prized data that is not filtered through the lens of assumptions, through ideas, through theories, through traditional lenses or constructs that the person has been told, read, or learned about, whether from a particular horseperson, a particular indoctrination, a particular approach of horsemanship, or even scientific theory.

Every particular approach with horses, brings its own set of principles, theories, and practices (including equipment and tack requirements or preferences), and ultimately, a specific understanding of horses. This means that when we use a particular approach (principles, theories, practices) exclusively, as a *blanket approach to everything we do with horses* it will shape how we perceive, think about, approach, request (or demand) and generally behave with horses. It will also inform what we can see and what we expect from horses. When we become married to any one approach exclusively, we are actually using the theories of yesterday (or last week, last year, 10 years ago, 50 years ago, or hundreds of years ago), as we were taught through the knowledge or practice. We are actually out of touch with reality, as we are hijacked by thought, reflection and assumption (theory). Here, we are (in a purer form) no longer in the present moment, aware, observing and tracking the phenomena, with an openness that requires a capacity to *not know*.

When we approach the other, with an attitude of not-knowing, getting more fundamentally curious about the *unfolding phenomenology* of the other, *without the theories* (frameworks, maps, or assumptions it requires), only then can we have a chance to be in touch with reality and truly learn! Of course, as humans we have the limitation of never truly being able to be objective, but, intentionally attempting to!

The I-Thou horseperson always prioritises the horse's non-verbal phenomena across the whole range of communications, and movement, and functioning over and above any theories, assumptions, labels, and traditions.

This is incredibly difficult for people who have spent 1 to 50 years honing their craft through a particular theoretical lens and have a particular way of thinking, a set of constructs and maps that act as a lens in which they perceive and interpret everything they're seeing. I find this happens a lot (people find it incredibly challenging and difficult) when I ask people to sit and observe a horse or observe the herd and then share their observation statements in the spirit of the phenomenological method of inquiry. This means, in the spirit of tracking the phenomena and the data only. (So, asking for description and descriptive observations only). Most people struggle and provide interpretations that are fed through a particular lens.

Examples of such interpretive observation statements include:

- I can see that horse is the boss.
- I can see this horse is the lead mare, who is higher up in the pecking order, and is telling the Palomino horse to get away.
- I can see the Black Horse is most likely the alpha and likes to dominate the other horses.
- The bigger chestnut does not like the smaller chestnut horse.
- The horses are struggling with this man-made herd, because it's not a natural herd.
- This horse feels left out.

All these comments include assumption, interpretation, projection, opinion or theory. This is what is getting in the way of or acting as a block for the person to actually observe, see and track what is *actually* happening in the present moment for the horses.

Let's go over the four attitudes and skills of the phenomenological horse person.

1. **Active Curiosity** - I have mentioned this a lot already, the horse person uses their active curiosity; an open, spacious, fascination in the horse's subjective experience, tendencies, movements and relational exchanges with other horses. We're looking for phenomena, and we are openly curious to the unfolding of the present moment's phenomena. This is a very different type of curiosity to a detective's curiosity, which has a sharper tone, is looking for an answer, cause, or assumption of right or wrong, good or bad. That kind of interest or curiosity is the opposite of open curiosity as it is still imbued by thinking and assumption, rather than an open aware state that is cultivated through presence. Presence requires regulated breathing, softness in the body, body awareness (that allows a knowing of body boundaries and separation between self and other), use of senses and sensing, all anchored in the present moment. We are not thinking and reflecting, where the mind is active and getting in the way of noticing (unintentionally). Awareness and presence support active curiosity.

2. **Bracketing** - The phenomenological horseperson attempts to bracket (put aside) assumptions, thoughts, hypotheses, theories, maps, ideas, reflections to arrive as the data or phenomenology as it is unfolding. For example, many horse people bring assumptions and ideas about lead stallions, lead mares, pecking order, vices, how horses should and do behave individually and

as a group etc. These assumptions and ideas block the possibility of actually observing the data or phenomena of the horse more purely, so one can arrive at the more specific phenomena as it is unfolding. Bracketing is essential and must be practiced, as thinking creeps in all the time with humans, who have learned and been rewarded for their thinking, reflection, planning and formulating. I say the phenomenological horse person 'attempts' to bracket, as given the nature of humans and the tendency to project and think, we have the intention to bracket, and get as close to the raw or pure phenomena as possible, knowing that we can never be 100% objective. Our observing of the phenomena and presence will always shape and co-create the phenomena as it emerges, to some degree.

3. **Description** - We use description and describing and aim to be as descriptive as possible in our observations. For example, describing minute data like the subtle shifts and changes in biomechanics or quality of the horse's movement, the subtlety of the shift in the horse's gaze, the lift of their wither, their breath being held or expelled with a rhythm, the orienting of the horse's eye, head and the neck etc. The description becomes really important as it is what replaces the assumptions of what comes next, what it means or what label we might attach to a certain group of phenomena. We keep the horse safe from our assumptions, and we try to be as purely descriptive as we can.

4. **Horizontalisation** - This skill requires the horseperson to attend to the range of all phenomena with an equal attention, not being skewed by an interest in one type of phenomena or action only. We are staying open to all of the horse's subjective experience, including their expression, communication and behaviour, and we're not just focusing on one area like the biomechanics, an exchange between herd members, the feelings of a horse or how the horse relates to the weather etc. We're paying attention to all the phenomena equally. We're starting to be an active scientist in the discovery of the truth of the present moment, as it unfolds in the data, the phenomena and direct experience and behaviour of the horse, while we are actively bracketing any assumptions about what that means.

We hold our assumptions about the meaning until we have most fully noticed, observed and spent time with the phenomenology of the horse. Only later, do we start to be open to tendencies, patterns, or functionality and cross reference with current scientific theories, knowledge and practice.

So, the phenomenological approach is our active scientist position, with a very particular skill set and discipline. I see many well-intentioned horse people who have not yet learned about being present and aware, and how awareness is fundamentally different from the activities of the mind (thinking, reflecting and insight). Awareness capacities are what support capacities for open curiosity, bracketing, description and horizontalisation. So unfortunately, the unaware horse people are unable to develop the skills required, as their interest, observation, and tracking of their horse remains attached or 'wed to' their maps, theories and constructs (they are unable to separate thought from experience). Thus, they are unable to put this to good use for their horse training or horsepersonship. Sadly, these limitations mean they firstly, miss the horse and their phenomenology, and secondly, the relationship is skewed by this undeveloped capacity and skill.

EXERCISE:
PRACTICING PHENOMENOLOGICAL OBSERVATION

Spend 20 minutes observing your herd. Use your outbreath to let go of excess tension or activation in your nervous system, ground yourself by bringing your attention down to the ground and earth and out of your mind. Orient to each of your senses (notice what you can smell, hear, taste, touch and see), and notice your felt sense or embodied experience (body sensations) in the present moment. (This helps you to notice where you are and end, and where the other and the environment begins). Now, intentionally use your:

- **Open curiosity** - feel like you have 'all the time in the world' (even if you have only 30 mins or an hour!) and cultivate and open fascination and intention to observe all phenomena of horse and horse-relating.

- **Description** - be as descriptive and detailed in your observations (and recordings, if you are writing) as you can possibly manage. E.g., the horse stood still versus the horse stood still for 7 mins, occasionally moving both ears back, right and left, with eyes half closed.

- **Bracketing** - bracket any assumptions, ideas and thinking (that gets you excited about a certain hypothesis for example), particularly notice the ideas you usually like to see, believe, make-meaning or expect. Say to yourself, "I will put you to the side for now, idea!"

- **Horizontalisation** - Be open to and attentive to a whole range of phenomena across the self-experience and relating of the horse (individual horse data or phenomena, interrelating between horses, and then broadly within the interrelating between the horses across the environment / broader field and so forth).

See what you can discover about the purity of the phenomena of the horses that are before you. Notice how easy or how difficult it is for you to strip back the interpretations and assumptions about what it all means.

Stay open and learn, for no other reason than
an interest to observe and learn!
You deserve and need support. We all do.

THE FOURTH COMMITMENT: TRAUMA-INFORMED

I recommend the use of ethograms to support the phenomenology-focused horse person to start to chart out, apply and practice observation, utilising the four skills and capacities listed. There are many valuable online resources outlining how to create and use ethograms, including YouTube videos from a number of universities. Lucy Rees has contributed updated information related to horses from her life's work within the context of observing and learning from her wild-living herds, supporting her students to use ethograms as a tool. Follow Lucy Rees work at www.lucyrees.uk.

Regardless of whether you use formal ethograms or not to support your learning and practices with horses, the phenomenological horse person must develop skills in the four capacities of open curiosity, bracketing, description and horizontalisation. These skills will be the foundations upon which you relate to your horse, as your approach, interaction, training and relationship on the whole will benefit. These skills can be used as daily supports to ensure you are meeting your horse's basic needs, ensuring horse welfare is paramount and that your relationship remains mutually beneficial and enriching for your horses. If you listen well, and skilfully, your horse will tell you what is happening.

This will support you as a horse person to stay close to reality, to stay close to your horse's unfolding self-experience, needs and wants, and their feelings and experience in the present moment.

It will reduce the tendency that so many people have to miss important information about the horse's wellbeing, stress signals, and relaxation signals and tendencies, as well as their individuality and broader needs - because they're getting hijacked by their own human thoughts, their own values, their own theories.

THE SIXTH COMMITMENT: SCIENCE

> A WHOLE-HORSE APPROACH TO GOOD, SKILFUL AND MINDFUL HORSE TRAINING, AND MOST CERTAINLY I-THOU HORSEPERSONSHIP, MUST INCLUDE KNOWLEDGE ABOUT SCIENCE, BOTH EQUINE SCIENCE AND EQUITATION SCIENCE, AS WELL AS NEUROSCIENCE, TO AID AND SUPPORT AN UNDERSTANDING OF HORSES, HORSE TRAINING, HORSE WELFARE AND ETHICAL PERSPECTIVES.

Additionally, I feel it is critical to note that science is a systematic approach that seeks to understand the natural and social world through obtaining and testing evidence to support known or unknown phenomena. Importantly, science is not a 'set and forget' process or a system of rules etched in stone, rather is continually evolving and updating as new evidence and understandings emerge. In relation to horses, science is a human map we have created to understand horses and horse learning. Remember the map is not the territory! With this in mind, I have collated what I believe to be the best available and relevant information, outlining what we currently know to be true about horses from a scientific perspective, from reputable sources. However, as time passes, I expect (and hope for) this knowledge base to be updated as our understanding of equine science, learning theory and neuroscience evolve. It is with this frame of mind that I invite you to consider this chapter.

Current science, in and of itself is not enough, I believe, to deeply understand and work with any social mammal (including humans and non-humans). Psychology, psychotherapy and counselling, must walk this line also, of including science-based approaches, evidence-based approaches when understanding and treating human social mammals, alongside phenomenologically supported, heuristic and qualitative research approaches, clinical practice wisdom, and client self-report - to arrive at ethical, efficient, effective and whole-being ways of understanding clients and producing outcomes and change. Not so long ago, science believed animals did not have emotions, feel fear, or experience pain, and therefore suffering! If an animal behaviourist or animal specialist works with an animal to produce change, without understanding, or including the animal's deeper emotional experience, their nervous system arousal and state, their experience of stress and pain, their attachment and bonding tendencies and needs, for example, then the result can be (and historically has been) disastrous, harmful and unethical. Luckily, science has caught up with the practical wisdom that always knew via experience and lay-persons phenomenological methods that animals have feelings, emotional states and nervous systems and that they experience contentment, joy, pain and suffering (Panksepp, 2011). But, clearly, from a welfare perspective, we can't always wait for science to catch up to practice wisdom! However, as we will discuss, there are endless examples of the opposite, where people have interacted with horses and trained horses (and animals) in ways that are informed by myths, traditions, projection, anthropomorphising and anthropocentric paradigms. There are also training behaviours and approaches based upon the human's unconscious needs, motivations and impulses, which has led to welfare issues, harm, misunderstanding, violence and death for horses (and animals).

I believe people who have not developed skills in the areas approached in this book – including capacities and skills in the areas of I-Thou relating, Values, a Trauma-Informed and Nervous system approach, Phenomenology and Personal Development (based on awareness) - are ripe candidates for projecting, anthropomorphising, and being swept along by ideas of their mentors or those around them of most influence. This has and continues to be a dangerous situation when people then choose to interact with animals and horses from this unaware and unskilful state of functioning.

Back in the 1960's psychology moved away from using learning theory and behavioural modification as the dominant approach to produce change in humans as evidenced by the "third force" movement in psychology and psychotherapy. This led to the rise in more whole-human and humanistic approaches in counselling and psychotherapy. Psychology and psychotherapy fields began to understand the intrinsic limitations of behavioural approaches, which focused on knowledge around and work with human *behaviour* only. The purely behavioural lens ignores or neglects other human factors or systems, including biological, neurobiological, attachment, affects and affective needs and motivations, cognitive paradigms and internal systems (thinking and belief-based functioning), and the inter-relationship between systems or layers of self-experience of the *whole person* – i.e. biological, neurological, cognitive, emotional, behavioural, and relational (social, systemic and structural) layers of human experience (and that is not including spiritual factors, as some people also believe this is a very important and real part of self-experience, human functioning, humanity and the world).

Horses have the same complexity of biological, neurological, cognitive, emotional, behavioural, and relational (social) layers of experience that science is only beginning to know and understand. One cannot understand horses from a whole-horse perspective if they do not observe, track, understand and include all of their layers of self-experience, functioning and relating tendencies. A horse is not just a behavioural animal, just like human social mammals are not just a behavioural animal. Both species are different, with different brains, cognition, affects, behaviours and umwelt (Saslow, 2002). Yet both social mammals have a wide range of intrapersonal (the *individual* horse or human), interpersonal and relational needs (the relational horse and herd, and the human in the broader context of social psychology, systemic and structural systems) that must be taken into account for a more accurate understanding of the individual and species (equine or human).

The above being clarified, we will now overview some equine science and equitation science that I-Thou horse people need to know to understand, interact with and train horses.

THE SIXTH COMMITMENT: SCIENCE

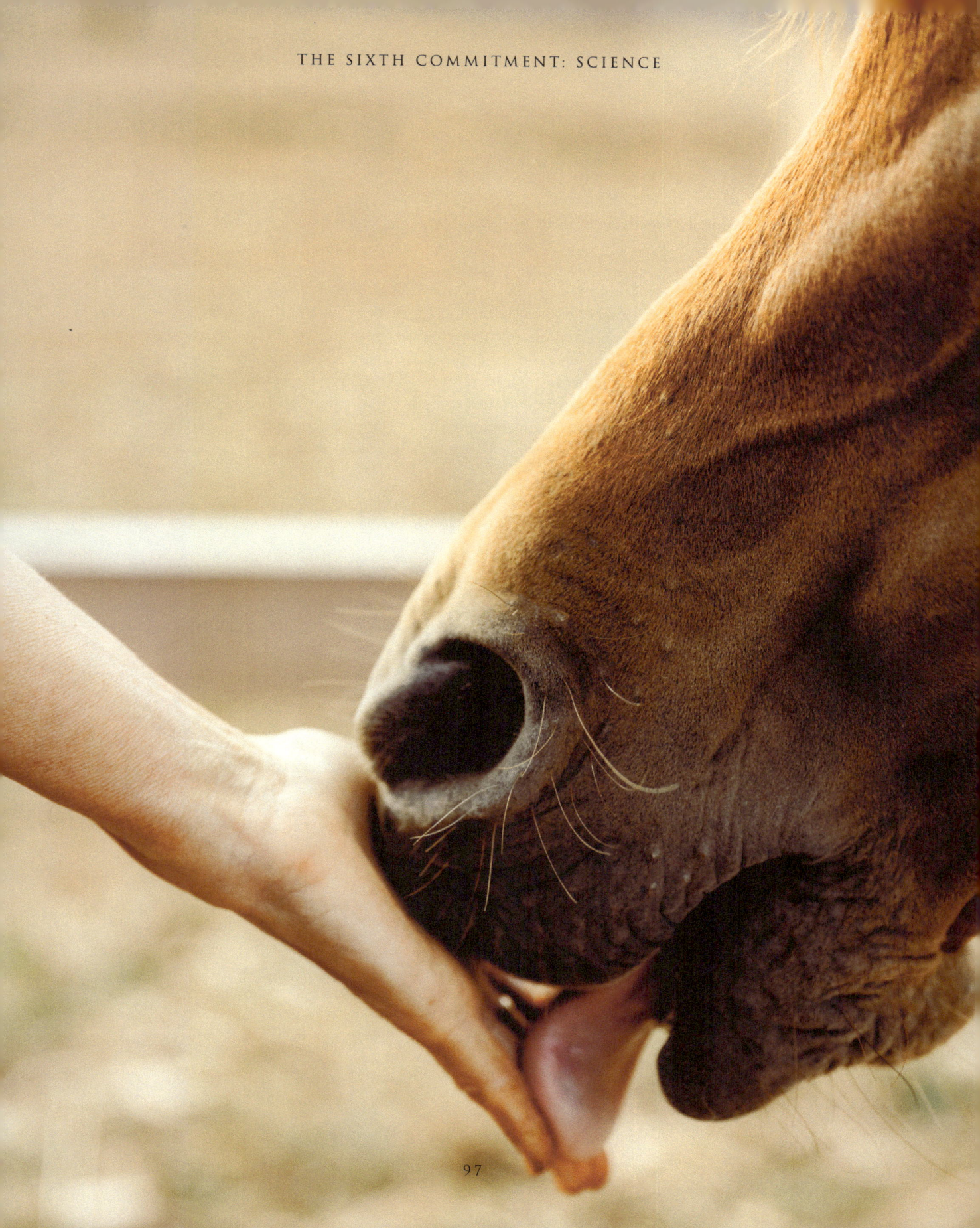

Equine Science

Most generally, horses are prey and socially-oriented animals, who graze, play, relate, attach and develop together, living in herds. So everything you do with your horse must accommodate, work with, and honour these natural tendencies of the equine species.

Ethology is the study of animals in their natural environment. Ethograms, as previously introduced, are an observation process and tool that include observation using an inventory of natural behaviours or actions exhibited by an animal, in a particular situation or environment. Ethology and ethograms support horse people in understanding equine behaviour in natural environments. Even though there are no wild horses left, there are *feral* or *wild-living* horses, who are free roaming domesticated horses, living in the wild or natural environments to observe and learn from. In this way we can continue to learn about horses and their basic needs, behaviours and relating tendencies in a natural environment, more closely emulating the behaviour of wild horses, rather than the characteristics and behaviours of horses in captivity, domestication and equitation contexts only.

In general, horses' species-specific needs include: (McGreevy, 2012)

Unrestricted Movement – where the horse moves constantly and the preferred gait is slow and meandering, often including grazing. Horses tend to move slowly unless startled or when young, or at play. Horse movement when being ridden by humans or lunging with humans, clearly does not meet this need for unrestricted movement. Healthy horses need to be free to move and graze.

Grazing and constant access to fibre - horses need to be constantly ingesting fibre unless they are sleeping or resting. Horses' gastrointestinal health is not designed to go without food for hours. Going without food for equines equates to fasting (where fasting means not eating for several hours at a time). Horses kept in small yards and stables have their movement restricted and they are forced to fast. This living condition alone causes or co-contributes to much colic and gastrointestinal disorders, ill-health and death. When living in natural environments where ingestive behaviours are unrestricted and all other needs are met, horses will spend approximately 60% of their time grazing.

Feeding and feeding related behaviour is an essential component in meeting the basic needs of your horse. Specifically, what you feed and what fibre the horses have constant access to, including the proportion and balance of the timing of 'hard feed' will set your horse up for ill-health or untimely death, or alternatively, a long life with a healthy gut! We as horse people have the ability to impact our horses' lives and health, most fundamentally, by attending to their needs, tendencies and behaviours, or not, via deliberate or unintentional violation of their very basic, species-specific needs.

THE SIXTH COMMITMENT: SCIENCE

Question - *How do you meet these natural tendencies for horses to move and graze for 60% of the time, in the domestication context?*

Answer - *by allowing horses to live in large spaces, with consistent access to fibre.*

Social Interaction - Horses are herd animals and isolation can be detrimental to any social mammal. When horses (prey animals) isolate themselves from a herd, this can be a sign of illness. Therefore, in a healthy horse we should encourage as much social interaction, social housing and herd living as possible. Human convenience is never more important than meeting a horse's basic needs. Remember, as a human social mammal, our societally sanctioned form of punishment for criminal behaviour is to isolate and control criminally sentenced individuals via housing in prison cells, where these individuals are removed from family, friends, and familiar environments, placed in concrete small rooms, yet have their needs for food, water, shelter and restricted movement met. Horses, being herd animals, have basic species-specific needs for social grouping (as human social mammals do, in different formations), and yet humans persist in violating horses' basic needs by placing them in unsuitable and isolated stables and yard housing, without necessarily intending to punish or violate horses. This is a perplexing state of affairs and the housing norms related to basic horse care and welfare must be attended to as a first priority, by all horse people.

Question - *How do we meet horses' needs for social housing?*

Answer - *By ensuring appropriate and safe pairing and herd living.*

Horses' most natural state and healthy state is to live in groups. Living with horses and having social interactions with other horses without humans present is a fundamental need (Ransom & Cade, 2006). In wild settings, there are different group types – the family or natal band (the group the horses were born into) and the bachelor band (usually younger stallions and some older stallions who moved away from where they were born and began their own natal band). These groups, as we have mentioned are called herds. What many horse people misunderstand is that the herd hierarchies, in fact, are flexible, they are not rigid, as once thought. Social grouping of horses developed as a way to protect against predators, thus providing safety in numbers.

THE SIXTH COMMITMENT: SCIENCE

Social Grouping - Social grouping meets horses' emotional needs. Members of the herd including stallions, mares and juveniles all have different roles. Stallions have high levels of testosterone, designed to support protection against predators. The stallion tends to patrol, move away from core of the herd and also drives the herd (usually from side or back or out in front). Because of the amount of testosterone, stallions are less likely to form pair bonds (i.e., best friends), but they can and do. The mare governs daily activities within the group and ensures no extra energy is expended on conflict and orients the group toward resources, even though they can also perform territorial functions like stallions. The juveniles learn social rules and social behaviour through play and living and interacting with herd members. Social order within a horse group is highly adaptive. It can change depending on the situation. It is complex (not rigid), and resource-dependant. A stable social order allows for threat to replace actual injury, so a horse in a stable herd will demonstrate less direct attacking, and more subtle communication. A stable social structure allows for effective behaviour in emergencies. Order or rank does not seem to depend on height, weight, sex, age, however more time in the herd can impact rank or hierarchy position. Higher ranking horses have more stress and more access to resources, whereas lower ranking horses have less stress and less access to resources. Conflict tends to emerge in herds related to resources and resource guarding (the value of the resource, and the ability to get and retain resources).

Questions and further points of reflection related to the science of horses –

How can we use this understanding and apply it in the context of domestication environments so horses' basic needs are being met? When we take horses out of a group setting, we need to understand the horses' behaviours will change, and that is why artificially developed herds in captivity will not reflect the normal hierarchy tendencies, ranking and resource-related conflict behaviours, as wild horses or horses in free roaming environments.

Horse people can assess the health of a group or herd, by tracking activities like rolling, trekking, and mutual maintenance behaviours (such as insect control and allogrooming or mutual grooming). The presence of these behaviours tends to be a sign of a healthy and stable group. A healthy and stable group will engage in activities together, such as pair bonding (dyads and sometimes triads) who spend a lot of their time together and are often a similar age and rank. In a large enough and stable enough herd or group, this is possible as there is enough variation for the horse to find another who is similar or a pair bond candidate.

Social distance or spatial boundaries between horses is important and normal. Depending on the scarcity of forage, the social distance of horses in a group may extend to fifty metres. If something threatening happens, the social distance rapidly reduces. This is a function of a group of prey animals. The horses with affiliations or pair bonds tend to have closer personal space requirements (as would be expected) of 1.5 metres or much less if they are mutually grooming.

Affiliations or bonding cannot be imposed on horses simply by putting them next to each other in the yard, paddock or stable fenced next door as they cannot form proper bonds, affiliations and carry out social behaviours and social grooming.

Conflict related behaviours are referred to in equine science as agonistic behaviours. These behaviours are associated with aggression, protest, threat, appeasement, defence and avoidance. They are the behaviours utilised in navigating negotiations and interactions with other horses. The behaviours serve to escalate conflict, establish rank, or maintain homeostasis. Higher ranked horses do not always display aggressive behaviour to lower ranked horses. It varies with each interaction as their interactions are complex. Other behaviours such as avoidance, deference, and withdrawal (submission) are natural behaviours. Thus, turning the head away is a clear signal that a horse does not want to engage, as is moving away. A horse exposing the sclera (the white of the eye) is a typical behaviour when they are unable to move away and do not want to engage. The jaw movement of licking and chewing is a behaviour that occurs post-stress. The stress may be mild or intense, but all are activating of the nervous system. Horses display a lick and chew, and commonly a snort, once the stressful stimuli, event or situation recedes or has dissipated, so the behaviours are designed to release stress.

> *Horses will use these behaviours in interactions with people, and it is important not to misunderstand the horses licking and chewing as feeling relaxed, rather, a release of stress through the jaw.*

Through understanding how social behaviour, social order and social hierarchies occur in free roaming horses, we can give more consideration and thoughtful planning to the social groups or herds of our own horses. This in turn brings the opportunities to reduce ill-health and welfare-related problems that will develop over time into stereotypies or "vices", which unfortunately give the impression that it is an individual horse behaviour problem, rather than a product of the violation of a horse's species- specific needs (for appropriate shelter housing, social grouping, movement or grazing), ongoing stressors in captivity or traumatic incidents either related or unrelated to horse training.

Observing horses in free roaming environments has challenged many other common horsepersonship ideas and traditional ways of thinking about horses including - the idea of 'dominance theory' or 'leadership theory', 'join up' or 'round yard' or 'round pen' approaches, the notions of 'respect', 'predator models' and 'conspecific models.' For example, behaviours in confined areas such as round yards and round pens (and join-up) may be context specific and may rely on negative reinforcement. This is an unnatural setting (round yard, where the horse cannot flee from or take refuge in the corners), is a form of entrapment, however it is framed by certain theories and horse practices as evidence of the horse feeling *safety, trust and willingness*, as the horse steps towards the person in the centre of the yard or pen. The terms, principles and practices such as Respect principles (where the horse apparently learns to cognitively honour the person) Predator theories (where horses perceive humans as predators) and Conspecific models and Leadership approaches (where humans are apparently viewed by horses as another horse, and as a dominant horse or leader horse, such as a stallion) are human concepts and constructs, and have no or little evidence at this time.

Communications, Horse Behaviour and Needs

Subtle Communication

Since horses can detect small movements with their vision, nuances in communication can be subtle and difficult for humans to see. This is an anti-predator strategy that works in their favour; using subtle signs with one another to communicate. Important places to look for a horse's communication signals are their head, ears, neck (position) and tail. Horses do not communicate vocally very often due to being a prey species. The jerky movements a frightened horse displays are means to alert conspecifics (other horses) and confound predators. So, this is an evolutionary social and anti-predator strategy.

Aggression and Alarm

In horses, aggression and alarm can look similar. Behaviours of the mouth can help humans distinguish between the two. Head lowering and lip licking (often called licking and chewing) can be a sign of conflict (that a conflict has happened and is a horse's way of processing stress). Snapping of the mouth by young horses toward conspecifics (and also sometimes humans) may be a less refined way of communicating submission. Young horses do this to signal a submission or a way of saying, "I'm just small," via a behaviour called gumming. Tension in the muscles of the head can be a sign of pain even though lips can be relaxed (covering the teeth) at the same time.

Equine Pain Face

The Equine Pain Face (Gleerup et al., 2015) describes the characteristics of Pain Face as being asymmetrical/low ears, angled eye (triangular shape), withdrawn and tense stare, nostrils that are more square than they are round (tense), tension of the muzzle and tension of the mimic muscles (side of face, base of neck).

Tail movements

Tail swishing can be a sign of irritation and signifies a state of conflict, or the horse could be swatting flies. Context is important. Tail swishing can occur if a horse is receiving mixed signals, perhaps from a human. It is not only a visual cue but also an auditory cue.

Sounds of communication

Neigh - used to locate and contact affiliates. Used to find out who horses are and make them aware of the horse's presence.

Squeal/ Scream (short or long) – agonistic behaviours (aggression, frustration). Often mares being courted by stallion but not gender specific.

Nicker – greeting that relates to something pleasant.

Mare and Stallion nicker – used when courting or with offspring.

Groans/ Grunts – relaxation or pain. Both can happen during riding. It is important to define. Colic often causes horses to grunt.

Snore – sleeping while lying down.

Snort – aggression, exertion, cleaning airway, stress release, energy release.

Tactile Communication

Tactile communication is very important for the wellbeing of horses – social housing is crucial for their physical and mental wellbeing. Horses need to be able to touch and communicate through pair bond touching, allogrooming and other communications and behaviours.

Smell

Horses use odour to identify others and to mark (faeces, urine and body scent if available). Horses will sniff faeces and urine. Ignorant humans may think it disgusting, however, in the context of umwelt, this is an important action for horses to round out their understanding of others and their environment.

Perception

It is now understood that there are large gaps in the scientific understanding of equine perception. Although society's collective interest in understanding horses (and many other species) more fully is now increasing, a lack of historical evidence, combined with the extensive 'expert' anecdotal 'wisdom' that exists in the equine field mean that much of what we know today about how horses perceive and experience the world needs to be viewed through a considered lens.

Vision

Horses have vision that is sensitive to dim light and movement. This is believed to be due to their evolution as a prey animal, making the horse efficient at predator detection from any angle, as opposed to having the ability to clearly decipher stationary objects (Saslow 2002). Horses have a wide range of vision, but it is more effective along the horizontal plane and horses must raise their head when viewing unknown objects to gain a clear view. This alone brings an understanding to the way horses respond to novel stationary objects, such as a lawnmower parked next to a riding arena, for example. A horse may shy, halt suddenly or raise their head quickly when encountering this unfamiliar object. The anecdotal wisdom approach may be to dominate or train the horse out of their natural prey animal response to shy, whilst an I-It or anthropocentric approach may be to label the horse as *stupid* or *stubborn*. In fact, the scientific understanding of our horse's vision may support us to lean into the principle of Inclusion, and truly feel into and attempt to fully understand the experience from the horse's point of view. If we are open and able to understand that a horse simply cannot see a stationary object clearly, or that they have evolved to detect and respond to movements, such as that of a flapping plastic bag or a hopping kangaroo on the horizon, we are better able to appreciate the lived experience of the horse and to find empathetic, I-Thou and species-appropriate ways to work through difficult or novel situations.

Sense of Sound, Touch

Horses may rely more heavily on senses other than vision to form a view of the world. They can hear at higher frequencies than humans and although they can move their ears independently, they are less able to locate the origin of brief sounds. A horse's sense of touch is extremely well developed, and they are able to localise a light touch on parts of their body and respond accordingly. One example is the way a horse will quiver at the shoulder when a fly lands upon their skin; they are primed to sense and, if needed, to respond to the lightest of touch. Additionally, a horse's ability to regulate pain perception is currently believed to be similar to that of other mammals (Saslow, 2002). This small insight into equine perception provides us with information about how our movements, sounds and how we touch horses have the potential to impact them in ways that go beyond relationship or training – it is literally in their DNA as a prey species.

Umwelt

Umwelt is an important concept that I believe dovetails nicely with the principle of Inclusion to truly attempt to understand the lived experience of the horse. It is often the case when humans attempt to interpret the behaviours of other species, that we do so through a misguided anthropocentric view or human exceptionalism standpoint. This means, animals can be labelled as unintelligent or unevolved based upon our human-centred values or in a way that sees humans as a singularly complex species, separate from all others. The term *umwelt* is used to describe the world as it is perceived by a particular species or organism (Berthoz, 2008). This accounts for the perceptual experience of that animal, including sounds, sights, smells, taste and touch as they are experienced by that individual, given their genetics, biology and unique species-specific senses. Not only is the sensory information available to horses different to that of humans due to biological differences, but the *interpretation* of the information also differs. This all contributes to the unique world view or umwelt of each species. The closer we can come to understanding the lived experience of another, the better placed we are to, at the very least, avoid harming the other or, ideally, interact in ways that enhance both their and our own lives.

The Horse Brain and Cognition

Temple Grandin (2006) speaks to some of the legal, welfare and neuroscience factors that relate to horse functioning and horse care. There are, "legal protections that apply to live animals that have a well-developed nervous system. Science has shown that animals such as mammals and birds feel pain in a manner similar to humans." Grandin goes on to say that the previously believed black and white line between humans and other mammals such as chimpanzees, dogs or cows in regard to brain and nervous system functioning is non-existent. Furthermore, the ways the nervous system processes experiences such as fear and pain are similar in humans and other mammals (Rogan and LeDoux, 1996). Grandin's view based upon neurological complexity of mammals is that, "As nervous system and brain complexity increases, the welfare needs of the animal increase and become more complex." She continues, "all animals that have sufficient nervous systems complexity to suffer from either *pain or fear, need basic welfare protections. Animals with complex brains also have greater social needs and a need for greater environmental enrichment*...Human babies are given full protection even though a newborn's cognitive abilities are less than the abilities of mature farm animals" (Grandin, 2006).

This very simple overview introduces some important salient factors related to horses, specifically, as a higher order mammal, where the structure of the brain and nervous system is complex and where the social needs are greater, this subsequently increases the need for appropriate understanding, care and enrichment-oriented environments. The fact that horses feel fear, pain and suffering, and have social needs for herding, bonding, affiliative engagement and play, demands a higher order care, welfare and enrichment protocols. This must be the priority of all horse people, and certainly is of fundamental importance for I-Thou Horse people who deeply care about the subjective experience of the horse and herds in their care or training.

> A study was conducted in which horses learned to communicate by touching different neutral visible symbols to tell the human whether they wanted to be rugged or not. Over the course of the study, the horses chose whether or not to be rugged and their preferences were shown to correlate with weather events. Overall, the horses chose to be rugged in wet, windy, and cold conditions and unrugged in nice weather (Cecilie et al., 2016).
>
> This study indicates that horses indeed have preferences, can understand the consequences of their own preferences (related to thermal comfort, specifically in this study) and can communicate preferences. Equine scientists and horse people need to firstly be asking horses their preferences, secondly, be developing sophisticated and rigorous means to do so, and thirdly, to be listening to the answers. Imagine what horses might prefer, and communicate, if they had more opportunity to do so. This begs the question, to all horse people – what are you open to hearing and changing (in your practices of horse care and horse training)?

Learning theory and understanding how horses learn

When we understand how horses learn, we have an opportunity to relate, teach and train horses more effectively, ethically, and with a deeper kindness and compassion that comes from understanding rather than tradition, assumption or anthropomorphising.

Many difficult behaviours in horses or behavioural issues that horses have developed are the result of negative interactions with humans, traumatic incidents with humans, or are a direct result of horses being kept in captivity and domesticate environments (whether paddocked, stabled or some combination). In these cases, the horses' living environment does not consider the basic species-specific needs of horses. So, understanding horses, who they are, what their basic needs are, and how they learn is a big responsibility that every person has when they make the decision to live, learn with or train horses (including ground based, in-hand or ridden training with horses).

Learning Theory

Learning Theory is the umbrella term for learning processes. Learning theory can help us understand how horses learn and can be a contributing factor to our ethical training of and relating to horses. Learning or conditioning in this context means a relatively permanent change in the probability of a response, either behavioural or physiological, occurring as a result of the experience (McGreevy, 2004). Sometimes the words learning and conditioning are used interchangeably.

Non-associative learning is when a stimulus is not being paired with a behaviour. Non associative learning can be either habituation or sensitisation.

Habituation describes the progressive decrease of the amplitude or frequency of a response to repeated sensory stimulation that is not caused by sensory receptor adaptation or motor fatigue (Schmid et al., 2015). That is, habituation is where a horse is gradually exposed to a particular stimulus, and over time, they react or to a lesser degree each time until they become used to that thing.

THE SIXTH COMMITMENT: SCIENCE

Habituation (the response decrement) is the result of desensitisation techniques (method), where something unknown and frightening becomes more familiar, known and no longer frightening, or neutral or pleasing for the horse. This is a big part of horse training where the horse learns, through safe, repeated exposure to an object or place, to no longer fear the object or place. For example, the rope becomes less frightening, neutral, or pleasurable, through repeated gentle rubbing of the rope on the horse's body. The horse preserves or conserves energy by noticing the familiar rope and responding with relaxation, over time with careful repetition. Here the human is intentionally desensitising the horse to the rope, by applying the stimulus (rope) gently to the horse's body, whilst also supporting and controlling (preventing) the horse's flight response or movement of the horse's legs.

A horse is unable to engage fully in learning unless in a relatively relaxed state and is within their window of tolerance. Learning in a state of high stress or fear can cause the horse to relate anything in that environment to that fear, which in the above example, will serve to increase fear response to the rope, or to you, or any other feature of the environment they are in, at the time of the rope training process. Hence, the horse person needs to be aware, intentional and careful about the process, utilising their observations and I-Thou relating capacities, in order to grade their presence and interaction effectively.

Habituation is one of the simplest and oldest form of learning and as a prey animal, the horse works off a process of energy conservation. For a wild-living horse, it would not be efficient to shy or bolt each time they travelled the same path and saw a tree flapping in the breeze. They may do it the first time, but eventually, they would get used to that particular stimulus and then could conserve their energy for when it is genuinely needed, to flee from a predator, for example. So, habituation is an old form of learning and is biologically programmed for horses. If the source of the fear or the stimulus didn't cause harm, and continues to not cause harm, it becomes neutral as the habituation occurs.

HORSES, LOVE & SCIENCE

Different types of habituation include:

Passive habituation – occurs when humans aren't present, or in a way that is unstructured. For example, if you had horses living in paddock next to a busy road or a kangaroo sanctuary, they would just naturally get used to the cars going past and the kangaroo movements. This is passive habituation.

Progressive desensitisation – where you gradually expose the horse to the frightening object or situation as in the rope example above.

Counter conditioning – is where an animal is conditioned to respond to a stimulus in a way that is incompatible with their original behaviour toward that same stimulus. Here you provide a different experience to the one the horse is expecting. For example, your horse is afraid of one feed yard that has shadows, and you place the horse's preferred lucerne hay in the shadowy yard with the gate open for them to come in, eat and then leave. The horse's new behaviour will be to enter the yard and eat hay, which is incompatible with their initial behaviour of shying at the sight of the yard or refusing to enter.

Approach conditioning - refers to encouraging the horse to follow something they are afraid of so you create a contradiction in their natural behaviour. For example, turning the horse around to follow the noisy dog as it leaves, in the other direction, instead of the horse walking away in the opposite direction.

Stimulus Blending - is where you apply two stimuli at the same time where one is known, neutral or enjoyable and the other one is unfamiliar or frightening. For example, you may apply disinfectant spray to a leg wound whilst the horse has access to their favourite hay or feed.

Overshadowing – similar to stimulus blending, where you combine something the horse already knows about or knows how to do it, with a frightening thing, so the known thing overshadows the unknown or frightening stimulus or action.

Sensitisation on the other hand is when a horse actually becomes *more* sensitive to a stimulus. Sensitisation then involves processes of teaching the horse to become sensitive towards an object by repeated presentations of a stimuli resulting in a large response to object or stimulus. This can happen inadvertently and become an unfortunate result of ineffective desensitisation work, where the horse person unintentionally heightens the horses sensitivity in response to a stimulus, action or object, by unintentionally frightening the horse further, rather than desensitising. For example with the rope desensitisation process, if the process is handled incorrectly, the horse becomes sensitised to the rope and develops a permanent fear of ropes.

Four Quadrants of Operant Conditioning

"Operant Conditioning, also known as Instrumental learning, is the major learning process involved in horse training and involves the variable effects of adding or subtracting wanted or unwanted stimuli to increase or decrease the likelihood of a response." (McLean & Christensen, 2017)

Reinforcement

Negative (Subtraction) The removal of an aversive stimulus to reward a desired response Example: Rein tension is applied until the horse stops and the removal of the tension rewards the correct response.

Positive (Addition) The addition of a pleasant stimulus to reward a desired response Example: The horse approaches when called for and receives a carrot to reward the response.

Punishment

(Negative) The removal of a desired stimulus to punish an undesired response Example: The horse tries to take food from the handler but food is withheld until the behaviour ceases.

(Positive) The addition of an aversive stimulus to punish an undesired response Example: The horse bites and receives a slap on the muzzle....

Overview

Positive reinforcement adds something to reinforce a behaviour (to make it more likely to happen). e.g., a food reward. Positive reinforcement can increase the horse's enthusiasm for learning and is becoming more popular currently, however can be less reliable than negative reinforcement. It runs the risk of the horse being in an aroused, activated or stress state, looking for treats, rather than a relaxed state, and feeling frustrated if the 'reward' is not forthcoming. Horse people need to be aware of the nervous state of their horse and that over-active or prolonged activation can be stressful on the horse's nervous state, even though they may appear enthusiastic, and in this way can contribute to welfare issues, with a heightened or prolonged stress state, if not used with care.

Negative reinforcement takes something away to reinforce a behaviour (make it more likely to happen) e.g., pressure-release techniques, where the pressure that is introduced is taken away, to reinforce learning. It can cause welfare issues if not used correctly. We need to control the amount of pressure applied and time our release so as not to cause confusion or increase stress through pressure, excess pressure, prolonged pressure, escalating pressure. Horse people must apply subtle pressure and the minimum pressure, within the window of tolerance of the horse, and release at the instant of the horse's response. Skilful (i.e., well timed, observant, clear), aware and choiceful pressure and release training techniques that prioritise relaxation and softness (in the horse's eye, body, muscles and movement) appears to work best for the wellbeing of the horse, in combination with positive reinforcement (that is assessed as appropriate and suitable for each individual horse). Uneducated use of pressure and release or negative reinforcement, carries the risk of welfare issues with incorrect uses of strong pressure, pressure that is not released, and pressure that causes pain, suffering, violation, trauma and abuse (including learned helplessness).

Positive punishment adds an aversive or punishing behaviour or stimulation to stop a behaviour (make it less likely to happen). e.g., Using voice to say NO or using a whip as pressure-based punishment. Punishment focuses only on what not to do, without guiding the horse around what to do or to the desired behaviour. Commonly, people are delayed in delivering the consequence. For example, if a horse kicks out, out people need to react in the instant it happens, with 'No', in the moment. With incorrect timing, the opportunity has passed, and the positive punishment is ineffective, for training a response. Unhelpful associations of fear, are easily be created. For this reason, positive punishment is generally an ineffective training approach for horses, animals and humans in general.

Punishment is controversial as it involves, commonly with horses, violence (yelling, hitting and other violent behaviours), which are clear ethical violations of another being. Often humans are anthropomorphising when using punishment, and not in control of their responses, perceiving and projecting human constructs onto the horse, like they are being disobedient, stupid, vengeful or belligerent. There are some positive punishments like the use of training poles, so horse has to lift legs and not drag them along the sand, that can be common sense and effective. However, positive punishment has well-documented side effects such as causing horses to be less motivated to trial new behaviours, creating a learned helplessness response, inerasable fear responses, deleterious emotional changes, negative associations with the punisher, learning deficits, PTSD and latent aggression (McLean & Christensen, 2017).

Positive punishment is firstly not usually well controlled and implemented (and more likely over-emotional reactivity in the human). Secondly, it is ethically and criminally dubious (dependent on the punishment utilised), and thirdly, in and of itself, is not enough to train a horse.

Negative punishment takes something away to stop a behaviour. e.g., remove access to gate, for a horse who paws the gate. This would be improved if replacement behaviours are also taught and reinforced. For example, a horse who typically paws the gate, is taught to do something else, with the energy, or impulse to paw the gate (the energy, tension or frustration that needs expressing), so channelling the energy or impulse into another behaviour. This requires creativity of the horse person!

Classical conditioning is simply the formation of an association between two stimuli. Classical conditioning occurs when something that was previously irrelevant is combined with something that is relevant, e.g., the horse learning words which initially means nothing to the horse, but then over time, when used at the same moment as an action, the horse learns to associate the word 'whoa' with a halt or stop. In this way the horse learns cues and aids such as gestures and voice signals. For example, when walking a horse, you could teach the horse that an outbreath means to stop (where the stop was previously established through pressure and release on the rope or reins). Now, a breathing cue is introduced just prior to the known cue on the reins for stop. Over time, the association is made where the previously irrelevant sound (outbreath) now becomes relevant and meaningful.

Combined reinforcement is the combination of both positive and negative reinforcement. In the context of horse riding and training, combined reinforcement is usually discussed as largely a process of negative reinforcement, with some positive reinforcement to enhance the reinforcing effects. This combination, when done well, has the potential to reduce any unwanted impacts of negative reinforcement upon the horse (McLean & Christensen, 2017).

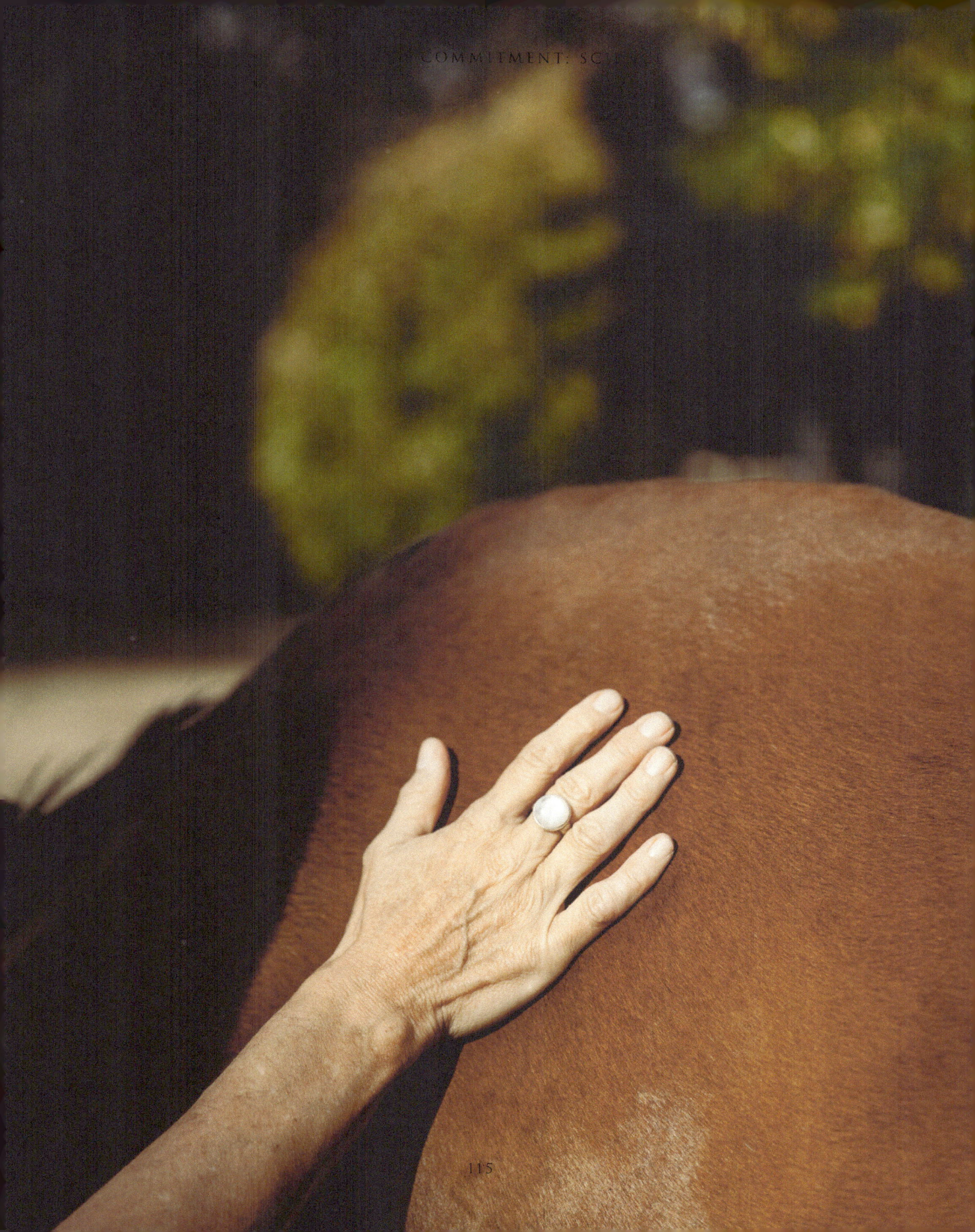

Equitation Science

Equine veterinarian and professor Paul McGreevy and ethologist and academic Andrew McLean developed the scientific discipline of Equitation Science or the science of horse training, in 2002 in Australia. It draws on equine science and behavioural science to elucidate the mechanisms of horse training and support the welfare of horses.

The Ten Principles of Equitation Science include-

1. Regard for Human Safety
2. Regard for the Nature of Horses
3. Regard for Horses' Mental and Sensory Abilities
4. Regard for Current Emotional States
5. Correct Use of Operant Conditioning
6. Correct Use of Classical Conditioning
7. Correct Use of Signals and Cues
8. Correct Use of Habituation, Desensitisation and Calming Signals
9. Correct Use of Shaping
10. Regard for Self-Carriage

A good understanding and integration of equitation science principles sits well in I-Thou Horsepersonship. I believe that principles of Consilience, Integration and Complexity always seem to be most true, in relation to human animals and non-human social mammals. Consilience is the linking together of principles from different disciplines especially when forming a comprehensive theory. Although the scientific method cannot theoretically ever be integrated with a humanistic, subjective or 'wisdom of experience' viewpoint, I maintain the whole is always greater than the sum of the parts. Any purist or reductionist discipline, in and of themselves, cannot hold all the truth. Therefore, even though I-Thou relating and Equitation Science do not live easily together (i.e., they speak to a different range of phenomena), I believe this integrative system of knowing, relating, practicing, training and living with horses – I-Thou Horsepersonship – addresses more of the truth of the complexity of relating with and training horses, then either can in isolation. Combined reinforcement and classical conditioning in an I-Thou system (including all eight commitments), is incredibly supportive for me in understanding my horses and educating my horses. Let me give a case scenario.

THE SIXTH COMMITMENT: SCIENCE

An example of combined reinforcement could be given by describing my current horse training experiences with my Arabian gelding, Jai. I have not ridden him yet, but when I purchased him months ago, the equine therapist I hired to assess him alongside my own assessment was unsure what combination of saddle and ridden soreness, permanent physiological damage, psychological damage or trauma were the cause of his dull eyes, depressed state, dull coat, clamped tail, tension through the back, shortened stride and irregular, choppy movements in his hind legs. Talking with Jai's owner at the time, it seemed more likely due to ignorance and neglect-related trauma, rather than abuse-related trauma. He acknowledged he had used an ill-fitting saddle, after which, Jai became unsound, and had only recently had a correct saddle fitting done. The equine therapist recommended a vet assessment prior to purchase (of course), but I decided I was going to buy Jai anyway, as I ethically couldn't leave him in the state he was in, and the setting he was in (as he was boarded in an agistment centre in a small yard by himself, with unclean water and limited grazing fodder). So, once I had seen him, I knew I had to take him home, no matter what the journey ahead of us was going to be. I scheduled equine therapy treatments for him monthly, and allowed him to join the herd of 11, and learn how to be a horse, in a social group (admittedly in an artificially developed domestic herd, not a natal band). Our herd are free roaming across large paddocks, receive good nutrition, have access to constant grazing, access to clean water, and four-weekly trimming with barefoot hooves. In this time, Jai had contact with people that was limited to feeding related and massage related encounters only, which meant that he was able to potentially develop a new association of 'human contact equals food and feeling ok' over time (rather than 'human contact equal pain and entrapment'). There have been many elements to our relating together, which include I-Thou capacities, contextualised within my non-harm, kindness, and freedom of expression values, trauma-focused care, observation, tracking and relating, and a phenomenologically focused basis for my interactions and use of particular activities. Activities (overviewed in the practice chapter of this book) included spending time together in the herd, walking together on lead, as well as more specific training sessions (based on learning theory) related to haltering, leading, saddling, mounting and dismounting.

In this last week, as a snapshot, our combination reinforcement has included negative reinforcement or pressure-release in-hand activities to cue a forward, backing and leading, positive reinforcement training activities related to standing still with saddle blanket introduced, then saddle introduced, then, mounting and dismounting, and walking through particular scary spots in the garden and the road (e.g., tight squeeze areas, and noisy areas). Our habituation work started with day one from desensitising him to people, ropes, equipment, areas and walks through desensitisation procedures. I use a lot of outbreaths, and, "Good boy" in soft, gentle tones of voice which may be classical conditioning or positive reinforcement (depending on the mechanisms for him). Most of the requests I make on the halter and rope involve the use of negative reinforcement where the pressure on rope , signalling a cue for forward, back, sideways yield, hind quarter yield, and following and changing direction is all achieved via subtle pressure (through human hands, eyes, body and heart, utilising the principle of **softness** through my whole being), and instant release with Jai's subtle (and obvious) shifts or changes in orienting, responding and achieving, the movement request.

It is exciting how far he has come. His coat is now shiny, his eyes bright, he walks or trots to me from the herd to approach me and my halter, he's allowing the saddle blanket and saddle on without stepping back. Jai has come along in 'leaps and bounds', as he is developing into a bright eyed, calm, but sensitive horse. We are currently at the spot where we are working with physical and /or psychological memories, blocks and pain that endures through his body, and biomechanics, once saddled. It takes about 20 strides for him, once saddled and walked out, **before his stride lengthens**, his poll lowers, his snorts roll out, his tail unkinks and his soft, rhythmic walking gait is established. His tail and choppy stride are quick indicators of stress, and body memory it seems. Jai will have his functioning reassessed prior to any ridden work. Slow and steady combination reinforcement training, in the broader context of I-Thou Horsepersonship's Eight Commitments are supporting great change. However, Jai and I are only just now at the pre-ridden stage of the work, and it has almost been a year. That is fast change for me, though for other people's perspectives, that is slow. Or certainly not fast enough! So, I think timing is worth discussing explicitly – I-Thou Horsepersonship takes time, just as good psychotherapy takes time, learning any new skill, or working through difficulty or trauma take time. There are no quick fixes.

THE SIXTH COMMITMENT: SCIENCE

LIMITATION OF SCIENCE

One of the dangers or limits of learning theory is that it is just that – a theory and rigorous body of theoretical knowledge, that is applied to living, feeling beings. So, we cannot take learning theory alone as the only factor to consider when training horses nor can we view the different quadrants of operant conditioning as discrete labels that fit neatly into boxes. Life doesn't work that way and, of course, neither do horses! "As Perone (2003) has shown, negative reinforcement and positive reinforcement can be seen as analogous in terms of the ethological theory of drives and motivations. He poses the question: "does the rat press the lever to obtain food (positive reinforcement) or does he press it to remove hunger (negative reinforcement)?" (McLean & Christensen, 2017). As Andrew McLean states "these quadrants or boxes are human made and there are no such distinct compartments in the animal mind. Humans developed these boxes to increase our understanding of animal learning. As evolutionary biologist, Richard Dawkins, famously said "discrete box thinking is the tyranny of the discontinuous mind" " (Mclean, 2022, page 83).

I-Thou horse people and horse trainers need to relate with the whole-horse, not just the horse-as-behaviour or stimulus-response mechanism. The horse's innate value is un-related to human's desire to interact, benefit or exploit the animal. Regardless of the truth, constraints and limitations of domestication and captivity, we must aim to protect the horse as ardently as we can to ensure its integrity as a social mammal, is safe-guarded. The horses' nature and behavioural systems - nervous system and arousal states, attachment and mental state (secure or insecure), bonding and social needs, affective states or motivational systems (such as supporting care-taking, seeking/exploratory, play, sexual behaviours and avoiding fear, rage, panic and grief), cognitive processes, perception- are all complex interrelated systems that we are only beginning to understand. Learning theory can only be as effective as our *current* scientific understanding of the nature of horses. It is best we stay open and ready to understand what we *do not know*, and certainly our ethical intentions to do no harm, do good, and foster the enrichment of all horses in domestication or captivity environments is our safest bet. Let's stay open, humble and ready to learn, so we can in turn provide our horses the safest environment possible.

Practice & Discipline

THE SEVENTH COMMITMENT: PRACTICE & DISCIPLINE

> I AM GOING TO USE THIS CHAPTER TO OVERVIEW SOME OF THE MORE USEFUL, COMMON SENSE AND PRACTICAL HORSE RELATING EXERCISES AND HORSE TRAINING TECHNIQUES THAT HAVE PERSONALLY HELPED ME BUILD SAFER AND MORE FULFILLING RELATIONSHIPS WITH MY HORSES.

There are two things I want to attend to before we dive into the practice.

First, from the outset, I would like to honour all the horse people I have met, whose books I have read, and learned something from. This way I give thanks, regardless of what I learned and what I agree with, disagree with, or continue to utilise in my current horsepersonship or horse training. You have all taught me many things of which I am grateful.

Alexander Nevzorov	Leslie Desmond	Pol Blane
Andrew McLean	Linda Kohanov	Ray Hunt
Bill Dorrance	Linda Tellington-Jones	Richard Weis
Buck Brennaman	Manolo Mendez	Ross Jacobs
Carolyn Resnick	Maria Miliken	Sally Swift
Cherry Hill	Marijke de Jong	Shelly Rosenberg
Chris Irwin	Mark Rashid	Tom Dorrance
Imke Spilke	Mary Wanless	Valence Williams
Karen Rohlfe	Pat Parelli	Wrangler Jayne
Klaus Hempfling	Philipe Karl	Xenophon

Secondly, you will not find very specific, *how-to* horse training exercises or horsepersonship techniques here in this book. As I said, I will introduce you to some of my favourite ways of relating and horse-human exercises (at liberty, on-line and ridden), however, it is beyond the scope of this book and my expertise to train you specifically. For that, you will need to access new knowledge and find an I-Thou coach to support you on your journey. However, I am fairly confident that by the time you have finished reading this entire book, you will have more awareness, perhaps more curiosity and you may have identified *areas of interest* that you wish to learn more about. I believe you will likely understand yourself as a horseperson (a person in relationship with a horse) more fully, including your strengths and under-developed areas of knowledge and skill. You will have plenty of creative ideas, and hopefully, a desire to learn and continue your I-Thou journey with horses.

Over the years, I have learned and developed certain principles and practices that have helped me come back to what I think of as horsepersonship basics. I have a herd of 13 Horses made up of purebred Arabians, crossbred Arabians, one Australian Stock Horse and one Friesian, so plenty of equine friends to relate and train with, each with very different individual tendencies, history and breed or genetic make-up. I am looking for my horse-human relationships to be beneficial to both the horse and myself. Even though I understand the relationships can never, in a very real or pure way, be equal and mutually beneficial or consensual (due to domestication, captivity, breeding and genetic selection and more), I tirelessly seek to provide natural-like environments and opportunities for degrees of equality, mutuality, consent, choice and agency, where and whenever I can. This is an ongoing commitment to extend myself, my relationships, my facilities, my financial capacities, more creative means and so forth, in the service of this intention, towards an approximation of mutuality, and the welfare and wellbeing of the whole horse.

I am always looking to honour the species and herd needs as a whole, and the breed-related and individual needs of each horse, alongside my own needs for safe and intimate inter-species relationship. I am looking to retain the integrity, individuality and expression of each of my horses, including their view, motivations, tendencies, agency and choice about what they prefer to do and not to do (related to interacting with myself and other people or not, liberty opportunities, on-line or groundwork, and ridden work).

I try to retain a sense of play and relaxation as the overriding principles guiding our interactions, unless it's a matter of medical or other emergency or safety. My intention is to always allow each horse to shape or co-develop what that horse-human interaction looks like and entails.

I am also mindful that safe, intimate long-term relationships are developed over *time*, where it *feels good* (on the whole) to be with the other.

Time, practice, and commitment are not very appealing to people looking for joyrides, one-sided pleasure, status, achievement or distraction (from other difficult life circumstances or people), or for people who have not developed the capacity for empathy, empathic attunement or care for other human mammals and non-human mammals in general.

Over the last 23 years it has been the practice of loving and empathic attitudes and behaviours (the I-Thou capacities and skills) over time that have strengthened my relationships. Safe, ethical and mutually beneficial horse-human relationships demand a lot of *practice*, if you wish to support and train your horse to become a safe, relaxed and strong, riding friend, among other ways of being together. Thinking or cognising it and *experientially practicing* it, are two very different and separate (though of course interconnected) phenomena! I personally use many of the skills and commitments I have presented so far in this book as the broader container and context, if you like, from which to include equine science and equitation science knowledge and skills, which then in turn support my practice and discipline (relating and training) with horses. From an equitation science or learning theory perspective, I utilise combination reinforcement principles (both negative reinforcement and positive reinforcement), classical conditioning (e.g., associative learning and verbal communication) and non-associative learning (e.g., systematic desensitisation, counter-conditioning, approach-conditioning and gradual-habituation), to support my what and how in practice with horses. I do this, of course, in the broader container of the I-Thou Horsepersonship eight commitments.

As I have said earlier, the commitments of I-Thou Horsepersonship do not necessarily truly 'integrate', but rather live side by side in a broader *version of consilience* (i.e., looking for solutions or comprehensive theory, in an inclusive way, across and inclusive of different disciplines or perspectives, rather than seeking agreement or integration, per se). Each commitment and discipline can contribute in a valuable way to understanding, relating and training with the 'whole horse', and none of the commitments in isolation addresses everything. In this way I am proposing a 'dialogue between' the different views or disciplines, that can be most skillful and most beneficial for the horses. I base my Life's Work in all specialist areas on what I have *personally (experientially) found to be helpful, effective and makes sense*, rather than purely taking on other people's ideas (including schools of thought and disciplines). This has worked well for me so far, and helped me to stay open, to embracing not knowing, being curious, and continuous learning.

Each I-Thou Horsepersonship commitment is a separate deep dive or speciality area, so I highly recommend you identify your strengths and existing knowledge and skill, and focus on exploring and developing the 'under-developed' skills or what I like to call 'growth edges'. Your growth edges will require intention, commitment, more reading, coaching, therapy, courses of study or training, specifically related to each of the growth edges you identify. Get the support you need, and take the time you need, for developing those specific skills and knowledge.

It takes years to lay down solid foundations for inter-species relating that include complex learning and creative expression. It took me 15 years to develop the safe, intimate connection that I was truly seeking, only to find that my wonderful mare was now too old and was needing a peaceful herd retirement (which she is enjoying today in her thirties). So, in fact, the special meditative bareback rides in the bush we had worked towards (over years of learning together) were much shorter lived than I had hoped or expected! Now, I find myself starting all over again with new equine friends, and rediscovering the truth - there is no shortcut in developing the safe, soft and intimate, long term horse-human relationships that I have experienced, and am now again seeking (which also includes riding out on forest trails).

What I notice in myself, and in so many people is a tendency to look for quick fixes or solutions that take the shortest amount of time possible (to achieve specific outcomes or behavioural changes in horse learning or horse behaviour). This mirrors the tendency of the Western world, which generally tends to look for quick fixes, in tight timeframes before moving along to the next thing, wanting more, seeking more... more distraction, novelty or complexity, in order to retain interest.

This reminds me only that I wish to do the very opposite!

Good horsepersonship takes time, takes care and takes continual learning over the longer-term. This is the way to build strong foundations safely and surely in horse-human relationships. So, I go slow, I take good care, and review, relearn and recommit to 'the basics' in this next life-chapter with my newer and younger equine friends.

I offer some of my favourite horse activities and training exercises below, to support you to return to, and relish in the basics with your horses.

Generally, I believe it is better to try and take care of as many things as you can at home, in a horse's home environment, rather than sending horses away to be trained, where at all possible. This means the human must learn more, take more responsibility to learn new things to support their horse's learning. Receiving support from visiting experts (in various fields of equine related practices) and specific help on site at home reduces some of the change or stress for many horses. I believe many people can underestimate the stress (and sometimes trauma) involved for some individual horses in being sent away for training to be started under saddle, etc. Imagine sending your loved one, a child or partner perhaps, away for four to six weeks with a stranger to learn certain new things, only to find (worst case scenario, but not uncommon) they found it scary, the person frightening, the experience confusing, the separation anxiety distressing (from herd and perhaps you) and at worst, they experienced force, violation, violence or incessant pressure or stress. The difference being, at least your human loved ones may have verbally heard or understood your intention for goodwill and your intention that they return after six weeks. This would not change the stress or trauma per se, but it would potentially contextualise the circumstances differently. Horses do not cognitively understand this (given the different brain structure and mental capacities of the horse). Separations (from the herd and perhaps from yourself) sometimes need to occur, but can be minimised, mediated or avoided, where possible. It can be well planned and carefully decided. At the very least, people need to put themselves in the shoes or hooves (or umwelt) of the horse, to empathically and cognitively imagine what their perspective and experience might be. Some individual horses appear to tolerate the above (being sent away to an unknown human trainer and unknown environment, setting, herd or facilities), better than others, perhaps dependent on genetics, breed, history, training experience and individual differences. Keeping the horse's needs (physical, physiological, psychological, social and environmental) and subjective experience (as an *equine* social mammal) as top priority in all decision-making, goes a long way in steering clear of unnecessary stress and potential trauma (which all costs the horse, and you).

HERD SITS - SITTING WITH YOUR HORSE AND HERD

One of my favourite experiences with horses is getting a cup of tea and sitting in the arena with my herd. People who know me well know that I have many, many cups of tea a day, which supports my morning, noon or night-time herd sits! A herd sit might involve sitting in the arena (with the gates open to the paddocks, for the horses to come and go as they please). Sitting in the paddock with the horses at the dam, or sitting way up on the top of the hill, high in the paddock, overlooking the neighbouring farms and Wombat State Forest. Just being with and spending time with the horses, without doing anything, other than being together, sharing space and time.

Here, there is not the objective of observing the phenomenology of the horse, or of learning anything, or doing anything but spending time in the presence of horses, being together, holding space together, without doing anything in particular.

The sensory delight of the soft sounds of grazing horses, the snorts, the rustle of the grass, the wind gently (or not so gently) blowing, and the immersion in the herd feels so grounding and connecting for me. Often, I sit or lie on the earth (depending how close or distant the horses are), and I can feel and hear the sound of the hooves moving about on the earth, on the hill, and feel very much a part of the field. This inter-relating experience supports an immersion in my sensing being and an experience of 'becoming horse' (of course it is more like becoming fully human!), through the natural mechanics of grounding, breathing, orienting to my senses, orienting to the herd relating, orienting to the wider field, the paddock, the farm, and beyond, into the distance. The feeling of solid interconnectedness is a strong felt-sense, and very reassuring. It supports a coming home – to myself, to myself as nature, to the horses, and nature-based wisdom. As I hope you can sense through my words – it feels very nourishing and connecting.

This exercise is just a way of life. I don't think you can do enough sitting with, being with, lying with your horses as they graze in the paddock, or as they sit, stand or move quietly. It's what I love to do with all of my friends, my human friends and my non-human friends and family, sitting together, doing nothing but sensing and being. It's about sharing time, sharing space being to being.

THE SEVENTH COMMITMENT: PRACTICE & DISCIPLINE

PLEASURE-ORIENTED TOUCH AND FINDING THE YES!

The other thing that I love to do a lot of, once I have a horse's consent to be approached, is to move closer in proximity, is then to touch them in a very particular way.

I like to find where I can touch different horses in a way that evokes and provokes a pleasure response. So, I'm looking for their sweet spots. I'm looking for the enjoyable places. I'm looking for the type of touch that the individual horse enjoys, whether it's soft, light, or feather light around the eye, the nostrils, the hind or the tail, or whether it's more of a deeper massaging at the wither, under the neck, or at the top of the neck, behind the ears. Sometimes it's a particular itchy spot that they're wanting to direct me to through the orienting of their nose, or through their flexing towards the particular body part.

I enjoy just having that open exchange, where I'm discovering where they want to be touched, how they want to be touched, where they'd like to be massaged, where they'd like to be scratched or rubbed down, and just allowing them to show me, to place my hands and my attention in a way that serves their body well, and their mind well. They get an experience of being able to *direct me* and in effect control where I go, where my attention goes and how I touch them.

It's a really enjoyable way of relating and it's a great way to, over time, in safe ways, develop what might be loosely thought of as increasing the horse's window of tolerance for touch, across different parts of the body It's also a great way to increase their comfort level for initiating with you, using their agency and free will to direct you (a form of desensitisation that is not gradual or systematised, per se). Here, you build this strong foundation of listening, of saying, "I want to know what you want, right now." This is such a joyful way of building safe and trusting relationships. You're saying to your horse – I'm here to be with you, tell me what you want, and how you want it.

You can touch the horse's body, asking, "Do you like this? Do you want this? Show me. What about this?" All the way from the feet, the legs, to the belly, back, neck, ears, head, nostril, hindquarter, insides of legs, near the hooves, and across the whole body …a safe touch exercise, without it feeling systematic, objective, clinical or dry. It indicates to the horse, through your physiology, posture and behaviour, your intention to listen, for hints of direction and agency from the horse, an alert attention and tracking of what the horse non-verbally says and does next. This sharpens your awareness for subtle changes in the non-verbal communications and behaviour of the horse, and opens the non-verbal dialogue between the two of you.

It feels good and is very much oriented around the pleasure principle. When horses understand that they can direct me, and that I'm interested, they will allow me to move towards particular places that they might not necessarily like, and they'll tolerate it for a minute before they direct my attention somewhere else. You can start to introduce touch to sensitive areas, or to areas that have been previously violated, used as control, or misused by other people (in other places and times), so there can be a corrective experience, a potential healing through this pleasure-oriented desensitising and connecting touch exercise.

Sometimes the horses wish to mutually groom me. They invite me to groom them in particular spots around the wither, the back or the neck and then they like to start to groom me with the gentle rubbing of their muzzle and teeth. Some horses I have noticed can do that quite well, knowing that I'm a human (without much of a thick skin and fur) and others are too exuberant, so I can't allow that mutual grooming process. I always understand the gesture, and thank them for the gesture, and then just gently manoeuvre myself away from their teeth. This allows them to find another creative solution, where they can continue touching me or expressing themselves in a different way. I don't interrupt the mutual grooming intention and energy if I can, to alter the momentum of dialogue (which can feel easily disrupted or tenuous, with certain passive, easily frightened or stressed horses, at first).

In this way, some habituation and desensitisation techniques can start, gently in the container of the I-Thou relating principles, with hands, touch and proximity signalling safety for the horse (or not, depending on their experience). It is essential to keep a close eye on the horse's experience and any display of fear or stress signals, in case the process becomes sensitisation instead of desensitisation or bonding opportunities. I might extend the desensitisation work to include particular equipment - rope, blanket or flags if I am spending time with a horse who has a gap in their habituation to certain people, equipment, places. Habituation benefits the horse greatly, as they can stay relaxed to things that are benign (not harmful) in the domestic or human context. This depends on how the horse responds, who the horse is, what interactions they are having with humans (myself, my staff, students, clients or family, for example), and what would make their life easier, safer, or safer for the people who spend time with them. I take whatever time that it takes here, understanding there are no shortcuts. It all takes time. It takes repetition. It's about relationship, and it must be within the horse's window of tolerance, and overall, feel mutually beneficial. I'm looking for the 'turn away', the disinterest, the want or interest changing *before* it actually happens, and before the behaviour escalates into anything

overwhelming for the horse. That way I can ensure I don't unintentionally increase sensitisation, or release attention (or pressure) at the wrong moment, unintentionally reinforcing a behaviour like walking away! I tend to keep it short and sweet for the horse, where they feel like there's always a degree of interest and agency.

There are so many books written by experts on desensitisation processes, so I suggest that if you run into gaps or areas that need further desensitisation work (for the horse's benefit and for your safety) when beginning with 'sweet spots', that you educate yourself further about approaches that are gentle, sensitive and congruent with our I-Thou focuses. Previous trauma or stress responses you have inherited with your horse are now something you and they can carefully navigate together, for the good of the horse and their overall safety for the future (e.g., legs that can't be touched due to violence with previous owners or ears that have been twitched). Horses with areas that cannot be touched or approached may make potential future injuries or situations difficult or unsafe, for example, a horse caught in a fence, whose legs cannot be touched, or a horse who will not allow their face to be touched suffering an eye injury, requiring daily care. This is important part of your horse training and if you listen to your horse, they can tell you if they need more support in this area.

When practicing the pleasure-oriented touch, I prefer to be at liberty, in the paddock or open menage. And I prefer for the horse to seek me out, so I might go into the arena with the gates open and see who'd like to come and be with me and support that kind of a share together. Or I might move into the herd and then allow particular horses to approach me, or I might approach particular individuals and see if they want my approach, my touch or any engagement with me. I may or may not also include elements of positive reinforcement, for certain individuals, bringing along tasty treats, to increase the association between humans and safety, enjoyment etc. Some horses in my herd are not good candidates for such approaches, due to hyperarousal, hyperactivity and frustration with the inclusion of food based positive reinforcement or some desensitisation techniques including food. So, with these individuals I utilise pleasure-oriented touch only, and other approaches that support their regulation, relaxation and learning.

Making Requests

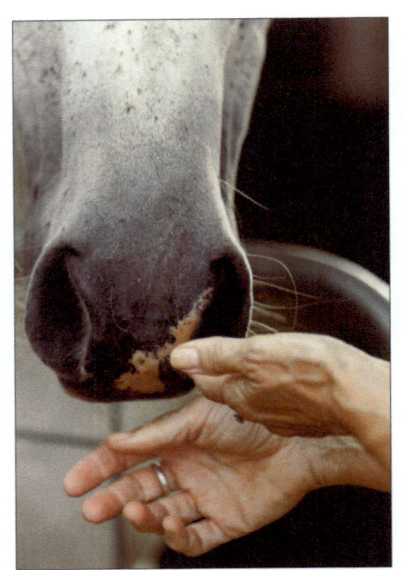

A request is a non-verbal question that asks your horse to respond to something you want, or you want them to orient to, become aware of or learn. It may be related to any type of request such as paying attention, moving, changing direction, changing gait, following, playing, moving a particular body part (like the poll, neck carriage or picking up a hoof), introducing new equipment, horses, animals, changing spatial boundaries, touch boundaries, standing still, approaching an obstacle, etc. Requests are endless really. Requests are a part of any longterm friendship or relationship. Usually in healthy relationships 'Making Requests' (asking or leading) is balanced alongside other ways of relating or interacting such as 'Being with' (being together) and 'Doing with'(doing together). Think about friendships, where the other person is always asking you to do something for them, and are never content with just being together, or doing something together and companioning (like walking or discussing something of shared interest). In these relationships the other person is always asking you to help, to try something, or to do something that they want. Usually, after some time, people feel used, and the relationship feels unenjoyable, unbalanced or one-directional.

Do you have a good balance of Being With, Doing With, and Leading With (making requests) with your Horse?

Requests can include a non-verbal question and dialogue that might start with -

Will you?

How about this?

Would you come over here?

What about a moving this way?

A request is something that you ask once, in one way, then listen, and respond to, once you receive the other's response. In I-Thou Horsepersonship *a request stays a request, a question*, and it never becomes something else like more Pressure, a Tell, Demand or Promise. This would require moving out of I-Thou relating into an I-It way of relating that requires control, increasing pressure and force. The request stays an Ask, it waits for the Response, and then you fashion another more suitable Ask, depending on the response or range of responses, and so on, in search of creative and clear communication.

For example, "You don't want to turn right," may turn into, "OK, would you orient slightly right." Or "What about if we go over here?" It may turn into another type of request altogether or acceptance such as, "Oh, OK, would you like to pause here. Thankyou. Would you like to stretch your neck out and nose down now and have a nibble of this grass?" Or "How about we head over in that direction, where it's quieter with less stimulation and noise?" Or "I hear that's a No, how about you just Look over to the right, but not walk over there?"

So, if we are to look at this through a learning theory lens, the negative reinforcement may pause its progression, in one request-response line of dialogue, and open up another line of dialogue or learning focus together. Here, you are prioritising the horse's interest, seeking, and tendencies over the traditional progression (maintaining the ask and pressure or increasing the pressure, until you get the 'correct response'). You are working within the horse's window of tolerance and with creativity, as a priority here, and of course avoiding training in any fear, stress or confusion. These nonverbal request-response lines of dialogue are designed to include degrees of mutuality and enjoyment (regulation in the nervous system), fostering the horse's exploratory, seeking and affiliative or bonding motivational systems or arousal, and, avoiding the fear, rage or (panic) grief arousal systems.

In the beginning with a newer horse, I like to explore very simple requests for the horse to move forward and back, and to the right and to the left, without any tack on or equipment, and later with a halter and lead rope. What I'm looking for always is something that feels sensible for that particular horse, as an area of interest or stimulus, if you like. For example, one horse might prefer a gentle touch on the chest to ask for (stimulate) a step back request, or another horse might prefer a different request. I am always looking for what suits the individual horse, given their temperament, history, tendencies, training, curiosity, capacities for play, fear, confidence, enjoyment of novelty or repetition and consistency, etc. With some horses, if I have a halter and a lead rope on and I'm asking for a flexion to the right or flexion to the left, they might need it in a particular time frame, for example, the horse might prefer a very slow request, and with slower movement and therefore more support on the shape of the head and neck as they're turning, because it's so new for them. For another horse, the request might be quite smooth and quick, to say, "Hey, would you like to look around here? Come over here." "Have a look here," or, "Smell this here." But I tend to want to make requests that include something relevant for the individual horse, not just an 'out of the blue' request or standardised request-response line of dialogue for every horse. Over time, the request-response dialogues, can be repeated across different places or environments, for generalisability.

I understand that when a lot of people make requests for their horse to come forward, move back, look, move to the side, look to the right, look to the left, move their head around, step over here, walk over there, trot over there, etc. they don't like to talk or verbalise as they make the behavioural request. However, what I've noticed is that it's really useful for me, from the perspective of congruence, to sometimes say out loud (verbally)

Would you come here?

Can you step back?

Would you like to look over here?

How about if you move across this way?

For me, I think it helps with the *specificity*, congruence and clarity of my communication and gestures.

It ensures everything that I offer is in fact a request, a very clear and thorough request that is 'all through' me (my mind and body).

So let's talk about when the horses say in their body language (non-verbally) "What?" "What this?" "Not sure" "No." "No thank you." Or "No way!" Or perhaps, "I'm not sure… maybe." When that happens, I'm going to check it out through a non-verbal conversation or request-response dialogue, with my focus, body, feel (tactile pressure or energy request) or use of my positioning. So, I might indicate or respond with another question like, "How about this?" Or "Well, would you like to go here?" Or "OK, well how about that?" Or "Oh, I hear you, it's a definite No. Got it, Let's…"

All the dialogue is dependent on the horse's unique response, affect, their window of tolerance, our trust and safety in relationship, time (to get creative), and the horse's capacity to tolerate variations of the request. For example, I might take this down a notch, and ask the horse something they already know about doing confidently. If I run into a fear or stressful response, then, I first and foremost go back to my trauma-informed *support tool kit*, perhaps using a series of outbreaths and let down breaths (snorts), using a soothing voice tone, re-focusing on a lower order request (that I can reward with their favourite positive reinforcement (feed, wither massage, touch), walking back towards the pair bond horse or herd if we are separate, etc, etc. It all depends on that unique horse and the context, and the settling and relaxing techniques available to me (in my support toolkit) that I know suit them. Effectively, I am looking to support a de-escalation in their nervous system and stress responses, re-regulating the nervous system to produce a relaxation response.

The key is balancing the amount of time you spend with your horse building the relationship through being to being, doing together, and making requests. Each horse will prefer a different balance of all three, however, I know from meeting hundreds and hundreds of students, that people almost always need to prioritise more time spent with their horses where there are No Requests, and more Being Together.

EXERCISE:
JOURNAL YOUR BALANCE SHEET

Journal your daily and weekly balance sheet of Being With, Doing With, and Requests with your Horse. Brainstorm ideas and actions to commit to a healthier balance for the benefit of your overall Relationship, over the long term.

Commit to a healthier balance.

The Approach and Halter

When you move out into the paddock to *approach and greet* your horse, you bring the four capacities of your I-Thou with you. Your presence, your inclusion, your commitment to dialogue, your confirmation, is expressed through your whole (mind-body) approach. You bring your values, your alignment and commitment with your values (and the responsibilities that these requires of you). You bring your personal development commitment to *being as aware, as connected* and grounded and responsible for your own self-experience, your impact on others, as you approach your horses. You bring all that in *your Way* of approaching the horse as you meet them in the paddock. This is no small feat, and this sets the scene for everything that happens beyond the halter.

As we discussed in the chapter on I-Thou relating, this will require the use of your outbreath and letting go of any excess tension or energy in the body. This will require grounding, centring, and anchoring through your feet to the ground and the earth below, to find stability and balance in your presence. It also requires a tuning into your sensing-being, your capacity to see, hear, smell, taste, touch, and a capacity to move out of the preoccupation with thoughts and the mind and into the present moments experience of what is unfolding in the here and now. Now, you are Here, to Meet the Horse.

Through your body, through your feelings, through tracking your self-experience (tracking with your phenomenologically focused lens), you are picking up through observation, feel and sensing capacities, *the phenomena of the other* (the unfolding phenomenology of the horse) including the horse relating between herd members and the environment. This is a skilful approach!

Your approach to the horse is not like a traditional or unaware approach, where you get out of the car (or walk out of the house) and walk up to the horse and just reach out in an unaware and ungrounded way. This is not an approach where you reach out to touch the horse or interact with the horse on "auto pilot". Auto pilot approaches can include anything and everything (unaware and habitual), including expressions like -

"You love me, don't you?""

"Oh, you're being naughty turning away!

"Oh, what's that? What a cheeky bugger, you just want my carrot don't you?""

"Don't you put your ears back to me, that's disrespectful."

"Did you get out of the wrong side of the stable this morning?"

And so on...

These are examples of the every-day, auto pilot (unthinking and unaware) human ways of approaching a horse, when someone is fixed in an anthropomorphising frame of mind, when they're hijacked by their human oriented thoughts and labels, or when they're unaware of their own experience, unaware of the other, unaware of the different species of the other social mammal (and the prey, play and herd tendencies of equines). So, many people without understanding and applying the first three commitments (and the skilfulness they require) approach horses in this way, with all of that unawareness, unintentional ignorance and baggage in tow! Can you imagine being a horse and having a human approach you, meet you, and want to teach you things, in this way?

The I-Thou horseperson brings their love, values, personal development, trauma-informed skills, equine science and equitation science knowledge and skills along, as they approach and walk towards their horse. They bring these skills in the approach, with openly curiosity in the present moment.

You bring an approach of "Hello! Who are You? What are you experiencing today?"

This is what is happening as you read the horses nonverbal communications, indicating how they're actually feeling, what they're experiencing in their nervous system, what they're noticing, how they're orienting, etc. That information and non-verbal communication is what will inform *how* you approach, *where* you approach, how you might introduce the halter, position the halter, tie the halter, or how you may handle or attach the halter. Watch. Breathe. Notice.

So, everything is done in a broader container of awareness - with awareness of self, with awareness of the horse's experience, and with awareness of the impact you and your approach is having on the horse in the present moment, given the environment that you're in (of course, including the weather, the other herd members, and the unique space around you). Your awareness and conceptual thinking influence your approach, and ongoing responses with the horse. It's fascinating, isn't it? So much to notice. So much to work with.

We start with that simple (but in many ways, full, skilful, and complex) way of understanding and operationalising the 'approach and halter'.

If your horse is looking towards you with their ears forward, they might be interested. If they are relaxed, with their legs positioned in particular way, if they're standing still, or just grazing softly, they might look up and notice you with a soft expression in their eyes. They may be expressing something like, "You are there. I'm OK with you being there." Or they may be walking towards you for some bonding, touch, food or, to place their head in your halter. They may be expressing something like, "You are safe and OK to me," or, "You are of interest to me." This is what we would want to see in the horse, over time, including a relaxation and soft body language, in the stillness, or in the seeking (perhaps the motivational system of seeking (exploratory system) or affiliation (care system) indicating safety and health.

We can guess that this behaviour indicates a degree of consent or "I see you" "I'm content enough to be haltered" "I feel safe and interested in you."

If the horse looks away, turns away walks away or trots away, clearly they are indicating degrees of tension, stress or a No, a disinterest, or un-safety. It may be related to threat and fear, it may be related to habit, it may be related to what happened yesterday. It might be related to you, and what being with you means for the horse, or, past interactions with humans.

So, you're listening and noticing all of this, and then responding to that response of the horse. We are looking for the Yes, in the softness, relaxation or seeking of the horse.

You now have a series of choices about how to creatively respond, with open curiosity, to the horse indicating stress or a No – with all of your knowledge and skill. Now you have more phenomenology to digest, more to reflect on, to then inform your next creative move.

Your possibilities could include:

- Pausing
- Retreating
- Stepping away and Reflecting on Options
- Re-approaching in a different manner, for example
    - Regulating yourself with the breath, grounding and resourcing, so your nervous system is more regulated and relaxed
    - Changing up the whole scenario by waiting until feed time
    - Waiting until all the horses come in together in feed yards
    - Waiting until a different time of day
    - Waiting until you are in a safe, enclosed area, and introducing desensitisation or positive reinforcement techniques
    - Following the horse and stepping back the moment the horse stops walking (negative reinforcement technique)

- Observing the horse further
- Dropping the halter
- Dropping the halter, walking to the (off) side, and exploring if a seeking or stepping toward response could be encouraged with the introduction of a tasty treat

The choices are endless.

What they do not include now, is an unaware 'bumbling along' on 'automatic pilot' (a mindless, unaware state) doing the same thing and hoping for a different response or a movement into a forceful, frightening, controlling, hunting or aggressive, "I will catch you, and wait until I do (you will get it)!" "You are trying to manipulate me, I will out-smart you." I hope it goes without saying that any fear-based, dominance-based, and aggressive approaches based on ignorance and anthropomorphising with horses are the polar opposite of I-Thou Horsepersonship and have no logical or ethical place in horse training or horse-human relating.

After you work for some time on your approach with your horse, and finding a Yes, for the Haltering, you will then be ready for more exercises together. One of my favourite exercises of all time with horses is to take horses for walks down the road and into the bush.

EXERCISE:

WALK TOGETHER FOR NO OTHER REASON THAN BEING TOGETHER

What is that like for you?

For your Horse?

For your Bond?

THE SEVENTH COMMITMENT: PRACTICE & DISCIPLINE

Taking the horse out for a Walk

Some horse people find this difficult to appreciate because they have assumptions that this somehow means a failure. It can elicit questions such as:

Why aren't you riding your horse?

Why are you leading your horse down the road?

Is there something wrong?

These questions are based upon the assumption that the horse is only 'good' for riding, not as a friend or companion walking alongside you, like other human or canine friends, for example.

However, for me this exercise is not only great for horses who have not yet been started under saddle, or are 'green,' new to you, or your property, it's also a wonderful way of spending time with *all* horses. You might have quite a comfortable and consensual capacity to be riding with a particular horse yet choose to take a walk as an important way of merely *spending time together*. Here, there can be space for the horse to be openly curious about the environment, about you, in movement together, and about the relating, when there is not *somebody on their back*. It's a different experience. Neither one horse-human interaction is better than the other (assuming the horse is not being harmed or experiencing discomfort, stress or pain in the ridden interaction).

Walking together is a great way of picking up more information about how the horse is feeling, how they're moving, how they're going, what they're interested in, and generally what they are experiencing in this present moment.

Some other information this activity can provide about our equine friend may include

Where does their attention go?

When do they feel relaxed and settled?

When do they feel frightened or unsure?

How can you support them, to stay in their Window of Tolerance in an open environment?

What is their rhythm, movement, biomechanics today?

How curious and forward are they feeling?

How do they feel about leaving their herd?

How do they feel about the weather?

Do they want to trot? (Are you able to accompany them as you run along together? Are you fit enough?

Are you interested in your own health as much as you are your horses' health!?)

How can you allow them to orient you? To lead and direct you?

What do they do? What do they want to do?

How can you support mutuality in the walking together experience?

What do you notice? What do you want?

THE SEVENTH COMMITMENT: PRACTICE & DISCIPLINE

This activity allows you and your horse to share the 'give and take' of being, moving and sensing together. Can you pause for a graze at a sweet, grassy spot, to give the horse what they might enjoy (or offer a positive reinforcement or counter conditioning (if trails are scary, and food/grazing is pleasurable enough)? Can you experience the joys and challenges of inter-species relating that includes choice and agency of both partners, and includes ongoing dialogue "What about this?" "What about we turn left here (as we usually turn right)?" etc.

This is one of my favourite things to do, to take horses for walks out the road and down into the bush. The sweet-smelling grass, the dew and waterways, the smell of the earth, and the eucalypts, spotting the magpies, the rabbits, the crickets chirping in summer....and the beautiful shapes, smells and feeling of being with my equine friends. Such sweet joy! Sensing. Relating. Training.

Aware Riding and the Mindful Trail Ride

If you have a horse that you have built a safe relationship with over time, you have taken for many walks, you enjoy spending time with, they enjoy you, you have started and trained under saddle (with or without other people's help), and who now regularly seeks you when you approach with your halter, says yes non-verbally (with the display of non-verbal communications and responses when you saddle and mount), you may be ready to enjoy Aware Riding or Mindful Trail Rides together. This takes a long time and is a skilful position to be in, as your relationship now includes a lot of familiarity, joy, trust and safety together. Your horse is strong enough to carry you (and your weight), and you have supported your horse to travel together with good biomechanics (including long and low or collected riding, where the horse can travel in self-carriage or with their back up and stomach muscles engaged to ensure the horse's physical integrity, alongside their psychological integrity is intact). Riding is a skilful activity, and a high-risk activity, so there is absolutely no need to hurry to this stage of your relationship. It needs to take time, to be safe. It is not something every horse or human needs to do, or is ready to do, or can do. It is a skilful way of being together. The art of riding is not something suited for people interested in fun, or joyrides and pleasure only. Rather, I believe, it is an incredibly intimate and skilful, relational experience. It's good to get support as you learn about the knowledge and skills required for safe trail riding.

There is value and beauty in many forms of riding and there are many places suitable to ride, including the arenas or menage, paddock, field, beach and some roads. However, it is the Trail Ride into the Bush or Forest that I will speak of, as this is where I have experienced many wonderful meditative rides with my equine friends. It is essentially walking into the Wombat State Forest in Victoria, out my property, into the roads, dirt trails and forest trails, that I most enjoy. The walk out is predominantly slow, but can include periods of trot and canter, as is mutually agreeable to the horse and rider. It is usually an hour or so, short and sweet, so my horse does not tire or feel unduly impacted (physically) by carrying my weight and balance for extended periods of time, and I feel awake, aware, and able to physically manage the movement and impact on my body, back and hips (as a 55 year old woman).

Essentially, I utilise the regulation, relaxation and grounding supports that you have been introduced to throughout the book on my aware riding experiences. I use my outbreath, I ground through the horse's body and hooves into the ground and earth below, I tune into my senses, and I track the environment through my senses, to stay connected to what is unfolding in the here and now, in myself, the horse, and the environment. I am aware. I am connected to my equine friend through my body – sensing the horse through my feet, legs, buttock, seat bones, back, hands, head, and the rhythm of their walking impacting and shaping the rhythm of my body movements. It is an awareness journey – awareness of self, awareness of other (horse), awareness of environment, and the sweet and dynamic interplay of what happens next!

Awareness is a better word than Mindful, as mindful implies reflection and cognition, if you are not trained correctly in the practice of mindfulness as an act of paying attention to the present moments *experience* without judgment. This is a meditation, in relationship. My mind is quiet. I experience warmth from my horse's body and movement. It is essentially an unknown, journey of discovery in the present moment together. This is what I most love about the experience, it's a relationship journey, and you never know what will happen!

The smells, the sounds, the animals in the bush, your feelings and sensations, the horse's feelings and behaviour, her attention and orientation, wants and suggestion. The horse communicated her wants via her body language, indicating, "Can we go this way? Can we change gait to this? Can we pause here for a graze? Can we travel over to the fence to see these horses here?" It offers endless opportunities for the horse to initiate and to respond. It offers a smorgasbord of opportunities for me to ask or initiate, follow, lead, manage change and challenge, go with, and have difference of opinion or suggestion! It is a true relational journey - aware, intimate, and unpredictable!

Trail rides are an opportunity for you to support the horse to use their body well, so they are not bumbling along, heavy on the forehand, hollow in the back, but rather, using their back (supported by their stomach and underbelly muscles) to carry your weight, with balance and straightness, relaxation and rhythm. This kind of self-carriage means that they are not 'in-contact' (with your hand, rein or bit/bit-less pressure on the bridle) all time, but rather, supported to carry themselves, without force or suggestion.

The responsibilities of the rider include not holding the horses head and body in a frame or strong pressure, as this would violate the basics of learning theory and negative reinforcement which requires complete removal of the pressure, and a release with the asked for behaviour, and the logic and ethics of self-carriage. It is important to avoid any unnecessary sensitisation, or unintentionally create a flight, fear or stress response due to excess pressure (and confusion). It is important to benchmark relaxation and the welfare and integrity of the horse at all times reasonably possible.

Attention to and awareness of the rider weight-ratio as essential for ethical riding, as is riding with balance, independent seat and careful aids (and use of the rider's physiology, body and posture) that minimises seat, back and body impact on the horse. Here, we are focusing on the primacy of the horse's physical and psychological integrity over and above the rider's wants or needs.

It requires a commitment to the use of softness (through the body and mind), and a valuing of *mutual* enjoyment, over and above human pleasure seeking. As I said, it is a skilful pursuit, and not for everyone. The art of riding is something well suited to people who are drawn to awareness, sensitivity and intimacy. It is only suitable, of course, for our equine friends who indeed say Yes, and have been supported and trained correctly and carefully, and produce a relaxation response under saddle, to our mounting and riding. It is our responsibility to look for the Yes, listen to the No, and to remain openly curious about the horses' experience, consent and communications to us each day. Given our bias to presume there is in fact a Yes in the first place, it is our openness and humility that are our best guides alongside education and understanding of the stress, pain and relaxation indicators of the ridden horse.

Listen to your horse well, as you will find plenty of people who will, unfortunately, encourage you to ride a horse who clearly says No, who is unhappy, who is in pain, or who is in a stressed, traumatised or in fact in a learned helplessness state. The responsibility of the rider is very serious indeed if you value care, ethics, and integrity. Listen out and look for any fear, discomfort and pain, at all times. Look for signs of relaxation, regulation, affiliative and exploratory behaviours. Awareness and openness are key.

Aware trail riding founded in I-Thou Horsepersonship, it appears, can be a co-regulating and enriching experience for the horse and the human.

THE SEVENTH COMMITMENT: PRACTICE & DISCIPLINE

As a summary, I offer you some I-Thou Horsepersonship Practice Principles to guide you:

1. Regulation of the Horse

Use every opportunity you have with your horses, to regulate their nervous system, look for their Relaxation, and joy and see if you can motivate him or her to seek you!

2. Affect Attunement

Track your horses Affective State - Fear, Anger, Panic (Grief), Relaxation, Contentment, Excitement or Play and attune your responses to meet exactly where they are at, offering soothing, regulation, stimulation and requests or communication from this place. Breathe, accept, allow, support safe expression or containment or support, from there!

3. Increase Affects of Care, Seeking, Play and Relaxation, and Decrease Affects of Fear, Panic, Grief, Loss and Anger or Rage

As a general guideline, this makes good sense for all social mammals, but it's not always possible. Also, play with horses can be very energetic and aroused, so requires more skill in the horse person who creates playful expression in their horse (galloping, rearing etc). So, support, co-regulate and express safely, as needed.

4. Freedom of Expression - for the species, breed and individual level

Who is the individual horse before you? What and how does she or he like to express? To do? To move? As an individual, how can you support the uniqueness if this horse, to flourish, develop further, potentialise?

Is your horse a serious female, who prefers to not be touched? How can you allow this unique sensitivity, her personal space, so she is honoured, her individuality is viewed as not right or wrong, rather just an expression of her individuality as a social mammal. How can you change your expectations and behaviour to accommodate who she is?

Is your horse a playful gelding who likes to use his mouth to explore his world, to pick up things, toss them, paw in the water trough, tap on the gate etc?! How could you foster his unique being, his natural expression, and tendencies, and look to celebrate his seeking, curiosity and courage or confidence to expand even further?

5. Look for requests and softness in all your initiated communications

How subtle, light and soft can you make your tactile communications? How can you use intentional, timely pauses? What if you whisper to your horse? What can you create together in soft, mutual, requests to each other? Look for his or her requests to you.

6. Commit to Dialogue, Conversations and Negotiations

Use your I-Thou skill of Commitment to Dialogue to have lots of conversations, about a lot of things, to meet openly in your difference, your challenges and harmonious moments, equally.

Lexy doesn't want to go into the yard today, to join the herd to eat hay. Ask her where she would prefer to eat? Offer some non-verbal communication to ask, "Over here? Is this OK? No. OK. Here? Yes, that suits you today. Would you like extra time to finish before the others come out of their feed yards? OK, I'll give them more grass hay, while you finish. I hear you!" This is commitment to dialogue.

This is the opposite of 'one size fits all'. Goodness of fit is an essential relational skill for all parents, people and social mammals. What skills do you need to develop in *yourself*, to meet the needs of this unique other?

7. Honour individual Boundaries and Contact

Always look to not violate the horse's spatial boundaries, rather, to honour them! The horse's individual needs, informed by their age, sex, temperament, and genetics are supported by your meeting of their boundary and contact preferences. How creative can you be, how flexible and responsive. One of your horses does not enjoy being touched on her forehead. Instead of assuming you need to desensitise her to tolerate your touch, what would it be like to listen to that preference, avoiding touching her on the forehead unless necessary, and, finding gentle ways to support her awareness and acceptance of the touch when it is required (e.g., for handling or medical procedures using sensitivity and creativity)? Desensitisation is not a requirement for all behaviours in all areas. Be sensible and kind about this. Reflect on how you accommodate for certain friends, partners, children etc who have different personal space boundaries and touch boundaries and stimulation or sensory boundaries. Genetic, temperament, socialisation, stress and trauma can be influencing individual tendencies (humans and horses), so, look to understand and accommodate where sensible and kind, and work carefully with ethical training and learning opportunities where it benefits the other (human or horse!).

8. Self-carriage

How can you allow, support and expect your horse to function in self-carriage? Self-carriage involves supporting the horse to find and maintain their own balance, speed, direction and posture. Not only is it an integrity issue to allow the horse to use their own body and not be unnecessarily pressured, intruded upon or violated, it is essential for ethical horse training practice where correct use of negative reinforcement (and the timing of the release) avoids confusion, stress, and supports the horse to experience a degree of control of their environment (the rider and the rider's aids or pressures). The horse's overall welfare and wellbeing under saddle is reliant on this principle of practice. How can you support the horse's self-carriage at liberty, in-hand and in riding? How can you support the biomechanical principles of long and low training, and, balance and collection strengthening, when riding? How can you support your horse to step into agency and self-carriage when talking a walk together?

9. Take Time – Trauma re-training and relationship building takes Time

Take time to build intimate relationships with horses. Trauma recovery for horses can be well supported by their basic species needs being met, fostering choice, and I-Thou relating. How else can you intentionally work with and release his or her pain, re-condition trauma memories, and foster relaxation and regulation where there was once hyperarousal, stress and a sensitised brain? How can you utilise habituation to set up for gentle recovery? What specific positive reinforcement techniques could you use to support the horse associating you with safety and pleasure? How can you communicate to your horse that you have all the time in the world together, to heal, in the container of a loving relationship, to develop bonding (and the human-animal bond / HAB) and trust?

10. Intentionally seek to promote the Healthy Herd and the Healthy Horse

Look for allogrooming tendencies, observe if your horses are spending approximately 60% of their time grazing in a stable herd (with suitable horse herd candidates such as similar age, gender and type of herd members available) and look for expressions of natural play (rearing, galloping, amongst herd members). This will give you the behavioural feedback that many of your horses' needs are in fact being met, living in relationship with you and your care. Well done!

Ethics & Enrichment

THE EIGHTH COMMITMENT: ETHICS & ENRICHMENT

Ethics

At its simplest, ethics is a system of moral principles. Ethics is concerned with what is good, right, and moral. So ethically, the I-Thou Horse person must consider:

Is this good for the horse?

This is different to:

Is this tolerable for the horse?

Is this safe for the horse?

Is this OK for the horse?

This question would be answered by different horse people in very different ways, given their principles, theories, practice, skills, and education. Is it good for the horse to be a part of your world and life, to interact with you, to be ridden by you, to be cared for by you? How, is it good for the horse? Physically, emotionally, mechanically (bio-mechanical lens), psychologically and from the perspective of protecting and honouring the horse's species-specific needs for herd-life, prey and play tendencies?

These are important questions that I believe, we must consider and fundamentally integrate if we are to build and grow relationships with horses that are truly of mutual benefit. It is the I-Thou Horse person's ethical responsibility to be continually reflecting on these questions in an ongoing way.

I-Thou Horsepersonship as an Ethical Stance

As we have explored, I and Thou relating can very generally be understood as presence-based relating, where each being relates to the beingness of the other, without any need to change the other but rather feel into the others' experience so there could be an experience of the others' subjectivity and potentially a shared experience of inter-subjectivity. I and It relating is essentially strategic-relating, where one orients to the other in an attempt to influence, change, direct, use or achieve something requiring a degree of objectification and using the 'relating with other', as a means to get to a greater goal or end, for example, to change their behaviour or influence the other to do something for them.

This inter-subjectivity between the horse and human is essentially what I wish to teach, to ensure the focus of our interactions with horses are relationally-based and furthermore, serve to ensure the horse's experience, feelings, needs, behaviours and consent are not missed, used or misused in the service of the human. Horse knowledge and horse training skills alone are not enough to invite horses into a relationally oriented encounter, where the 'live' relationship includes consent, invitation and an exploration of the subjective experience of both the human and horse.

I-Thou Horsepersonship has as its primary focus regard for the horse, his or her feelings, wants and needs, as the most important intention in the relating, relationship and /or training (in the context of broader horse education and training).

I-Thou relating is both an intention and practice. It is an intimate form of contact that includes an intimate 'felt sense', a deep attention and openness to connect with the horse, with no need or want for the horse to be any different than who she or he is. It is a deep reverence for the unique being that is the horse before you, and no need or want to change him or her, in their essence. It is an attunement and curiosity about the horse's inner world, an awareness of our shared 'being' (human and equine as 'beings' meeting) and an opportunity for an authentic and expressive connecting that can only occur, of this moment, and of this unique encounter.

When a person is practicing the skills and capacities of presence, inclusion, confirmation, and commitment to dialogue, the potential for ethical and truly mutually beneficial interactions are possible.

Enrichment

The I-Thou Horsepersonship approach also includes intentionally reflecting on enrichment for the horse-human-nature system. There is a focus on what is safe and good for all (ethical and welfare focus) alongside a focus on what enriches the experience for the horse-human-natural environment interaction and experience. We can undertake the activities outlined earlier in this book to intentionally enrich the horse's life and experience, such as walks on the trail, herd sits whilst horses graze at liberty and finding the horse's sweet spots. In this approach, I also encourage people to broaden the awareness of their impact and reflect upon continually enriching the natural environment, bush, forest, country they are living, working or engaging with (e.g. planting out part of their properties with indigenous trees or forest, building walking tracks for their horses to minimise impact on the land, or using particular arenas or yards for herds to rest and rejuvenate so the land has a chance to rest and rejuvenate from the impact of hooves and grazing). This enrichment focus extends the ethical lens to include, "Is this good for the horse, is this good for me, is this good for the land, and how can I further enrich us all?" Enrichment focuses on fostering stimulating environments that promote positive and nurturing expression in all humans, non-human species, and the wonderful ecology and ecological systems in which we all live.

THE EIGHTH COMMITMENT: ETHICS & ENRICHMENT

EXERCISE:

ENRICH YOUR WORLD

On a page draw out three columns, and give them the headings Horse, Human and Nature.

List as many enriching activities or interactions for each. You might like to get curious and see if any of the enrichment ideas overlap, for example, could a slow walk through the paddock be beneficial for you, your horse (relationship) and nature (you might notice different plants, weeds or elements you otherwise would not).

See if it's possible for you to undertake an enrichment activity from each column at a specified interval, such as weekly, and notice the impact it has upon yourself, your horses and the natural world around you.

Horse, Human & Nature

The Journey Ahead

THE JOURNEY AHEAD

Thank you for reading and joining me in this journey of Horses, Love and Science.

Thank you for being open.

I trust that you have learned something about horses, about yourself, about your horse-human relationships.

Where to from here?

How do you find an I-Thou Horsepersonship coach or a horse trainer who has many of the skills and capacities described in this approach, and is open to learning from you and your horse?

I wish I could give you some good answers, but the truth is that I find it hard myself to find the support of an I-Thou *oriented* horse trainer or horseperson. I love learning and I love getting support. Unfortunately, many horse people are stuck in their way of doing things, in this camp or that camp, this is right, this is wrong, do this and don't do that, and therefore unaware of what they don't know (about horses, about themselves and about relationships). I-It relating with horses is still the norm.

The good news is there are many kind horse people, and there are many people who are becoming more open to learning. Even mature (older) horse people who have been using primarily I-It Horsepersonship approaches for years or decades in their early horse training or horsemanship, are opening to new awareness, new knowledge and new possibilities. This is very heartening.

Trust your ethics. If you *would* not do a similar thing with your human friend, child or family, that you are doing with your horse (in your relating or training), then stop, and reconsider a different way forward. It is most likely that horses have a very similar experience of pain as we (humans) do, from the science (and my instincts and practice wisdom). Remember the horse's umwelt, and think and feel into their subjective experience or phenomenology. Your values of keeping your horses safe, helping them grow and potentialize, promoting good development (wellbeing and welfare) in your loved ones, and avoiding doing harm – will serve to keep your practice with your horses ethical and positive.

Keep searching for good support and coaching, and be brave to speak up for yourself and your horses, maintaining ethical boundaries on behalf of your horse. We are herd animals too, and we need support to learn.

Your horse's signs of discomfort, fear, stress, pain and trauma are not as easy to read if you are not looking, listening, tracking and being open.

HORSES, LOVE & SCIENCE

Keep your eyes, ears, mind, and heart open.

For the love of horses, their welfare and wellbeing as equines.

For the love of humans and our ongoing wellbeing.

For the love of our inter-species bonds.

For the love of our precious planet, the natural world (and ourselves too, as nature).

Meg.

THE SEVENTH COMMITMENT: PRACTICE & DISCIPLINE

REFERENCES

Bekoff, M. (2000). The Smile of a Dolphin: Remarkable Accounts of Animal Emotions. Random House/Discovery Books. New York.

Berthoz, A. (Ed.). (2008). *Neurobiology of" Umwelt": How Living Beings Perceive the World.* Springer Science & Business Media.

Buber, M. (1923). *I and Thou.* T. & T. Clark, Edinburgh.

Cecilie, M., Grete, H. M., & Knut, E. (2016). *Horses can learn to use symbols to communicate their preferences.* Applied animal behavior science.

Cozolino, L. (2017). *The neuroscience of psychotherapy: Healing the social brain (Norton Series on Interpersonal Neurobiology).* W.W. Norton & Company.

Draaisma, R. (2017). *Language signs and calming signals of horses: recognition and application.* CRC Press.

Gleerup, K. B., Forkman, B., Lindegaard, C., & Andersen, P. H. (2015). An equine pain face. *Veterinary anaesthesia and analgesia*, 42(1), 103–114. https://doi.org/10.1111/vaa.12212

Grandin, T. (2006). *Animals are not things. People, Property, Or Pets?* 205. New Directions in the Human-Animal Bond, Beck, A. M. Series Ed. Purdue University Press, West Lafayette, Indiana.

Hycner, R. (1995). The Dialogic Ground. In: Hycner, R. and Jacobs, L., Eds., The Healing Relationship in Gestalt Therapy: A Dialogic Self Psychology Approach, The Gestalt Journal Press, New York, 55-66.

Masson, J. M., & McCarthy, S. (1995). *When elephants weep: The emotional lives of animals.* Delacorte Press.

McLean, A. N., & Christensen, J. W. (2017). The application of learning theory in horse training. Applied Animal Behaviour Science, 190, 18-27.

McLean, A. (2022). *Modern Horse Training: Equitation Science: Principles and Practice, Volume 1: First Principles.* Equitation Science International.

McGreevy, P. (2012). Equine behavior: a guide for veterinarians and equine scientists 2nd Edition. Saunders, An Imprint of Elsevier Limited.

Panksepp, J. (2011). The basic emotional circuits of mammalian brains: do animals have affective lives? Neuroscience & Biobehavioral Reviews, 35(9), 1791-1804.

Perone, M. (2003). Negative effects of positive reinforcement. *The Behavior Analyst*, 26, 1-14.

Porges, S. W. (1995). *Orienting in a defensive world: Mammalian modifications of our evolutionary heritage. A polyvagal theory.* Psychophysiology, 32(4), 301-318.

Ransom, J. I., & Cade, B. S. (2009). *Quantifying equid behavior — A research ethogram for free-roaming feral horses.* U.S. Geological Survey Techniques and Methods 2-A9.

Rogan, M. T., & LeDoux, J. E. (1996). *Emotion: systems, cells, synaptic plasticity.* Cell, 85(4), 469-475.

Saslow, C. A. (2002). Understanding the perceptual world of horses. *Applied Animal Behaviour Science*, 78(2-4), 209-224.

Schmid, S., Wilson, D. A., & Rankin, C. H. (2015). Habituation mechanisms and their importance for cognitive function. *Frontiers in integrative neuroscience*, 8, 97.

Schlote, S. (2017). *Applying a trauma lens to equine welfare. In A Horse Is a Horse, of Course: Compendium from the First International Symposium of Equine Welfare and Wellness.* Scottes Valley, CA, USA: Createspace Independent Publishing Platform.

Siegel, D. J. (2010). *The mindful therapist: A clinician's guide to mindsight and neural integration.* W.W. Norton & Company.

www.ingramcontent.com/pod-product-compliance
Lightning Source LLC
Chambersburg PA
CBHW041535220426
43663CB00002B/38